Freedom, Responsibility, and Determinism

A Philosophical Dialogue

Freedom, Responsibility, and Determinism

A Philosophical Dialogue

John Lemos

Hackett Publishing Company, Inc.
Indianapolis/Cambridge

17 16 15 14 13   1 2 3 4 5 6 7

For further information, please address
          Hackett Publishing Company, Inc.
          P.O. Box 44937
          Indianapolis, Indiana 46244-0937

          www.hackettpublishing.com

Cover design by Brian Rak
Interior design by Mary Vasquez
Composition by Innodata-Isogen, Inc.

Library of Congress Cataloging-in-Publication Data
Lemos, John, 1963–
   Freedom, responsibility, and determinism : a philosophical dialogue / by John
Lemos.
      p. cm.
   Includes bibliographical references (p.   ).
   ISBN 978-1-60384-930-2 (pbk.) — ISBN 978-1-60384-931-9 (cloth)
1. Free will and determinism. I. Title.
   BJ1461.L46 2013
   123—dc23
                                        2012036478

To my wife, Laura, and our three children,
Rosa, Billy, and Michael

Contents

Acknowledgments

The writing of this book would not have been possible without the support and encouragement of various entities and persons. First, I would like to thank Coe College for providing me with a job teaching philosophy and for granting me regular sabbatical leaves. This book was written during my sabbatical leave in the spring semester of 2012. Second, I would like to thank the philosophy programs at the University of the South and Duke University. I was an undergraduate at the University of the South, and I did my graduate work at Duke University. These two institutions provided me with the background knowledge and skills and the passion for philosophy that have made my writing of this book possible.

In addition to these institutions, I also extend thanks to various persons. First, I give thanks to my colleagues who teach philosophy with me at Coe College—Jeff Hoover and Peter McCormick. I am forever in their debt for the various forms of support and encouragement they have provided over the years. Second, I thank my undergraduate philosophy teachers—James Peterman, James Peters, and, especially, William Garland, who was my advisor during my undergraduate studies. Also, while I am indebted to various members and former members of the philosophy department at Duke University, I owe a special debt of gratitude to Michael Ferejohn, who was the advisor for my Ph.D. thesis at Duke University. I have learned much from all of these teachers, and they have had a great influence on me as a philosopher. Third, I am grateful for the advice and encouragement of Brian Rak, senior editor at Hackett Publishing, and Robert Kane, who served as an expert reader of the manuscript, for their advice and support in helping me bring this book to publication.

On a more personal level, I am very grateful for the love and support I have received over the years from my father and mother, Ramon and Mamie Lou, and my three older brothers, Noah, Bill, and Chris. Finally, and most importantly, I owe the most thanks to my wife, Laura, and our three children, Rosa, Billy, and Michael, to whom I dedicate this book. Their love, support, and good humor are valuable to me beyond measure.

Introduction

Questions about the nature and existence of human free will are certainly some of the big questions of philosophy, rating up there alongside questions about the nature and existence of God, the nature of persons, the nature of knowledge, the nature of justice and the good life, and the nature of the good society. Questions about human freedom are certainly deserving of their status as "big" questions, since they go to the core of our self-conception and the status of our moral judgments. It is, I think, natural for us to believe that we have free will and as such that we have some control over our own destinies—the shape our lives take. Furthermore, it would seem that if we have such free will, then it makes sense to think that we are morally responsible for some of the good and bad deeds that we perform and that we are, therefore, deserving of praise or blame for some of the things we do. However, if we lack free will, then it would seem that we are instead something more like cogs within the inner workings of the machine that is our universe and neither responsible for our actions nor fitting objects of praise or blame. But in these matters, as in others, our commonsense ideas deserve scrutiny.

This dialogue is a beginner's guide to the central questions and problems surrounding the issue of human free will. In it the reader is introduced to the three main approaches to the free will problem—free will skepticism, compatibilism, and libertarianism. Readers are also introduced to some of the central questions and concerns about free will that arise within the domains of scientific inquiry and religion. The point of the dialogue is not to argue for a specific viewpoint on the nature and existence of free will so much as it is to inform the reader about the different theories on the subject and the arguments for and against those theories. In writing it, my goal has been to give a clear, informative, accurate, and balanced account of the central theories and arguments relevant to the subject. It is my hope that readers of this dialogue will find themselves better placed to understand and critically evaluate more advanced work on the subject.

To aid the reader in understanding the material and in thinking critically about the issues, each act concludes with a list of study questions and discussion questions in addition to suggestions for further reading. The study questions are designed to guide the reader in grasping the actual content of the key theories and arguments. In contrast, the discussion questions invite the reader to think critically about the merits of the theories and arguments presented within each act. The suggestions for further reading are not intended to be comprehensive; rather they are intended to expose the reader to various key historical as well as key recent and contemporary works. So much has been written on the subject of free will over the ages and just in recent years alone that it would be overwhelming to provide a comprehensive list of additional readings for each act.

The dialogue format seemed to be an especially useful way of presenting the relevant material. In addition to allowing me to participate in a long tradition of philosophers writing in dialogue form that dates from Plato and includes St. Augustine, David Hume, and George Berkeley, the genre allows readers to see in an especially vivid way how advocates of different perspectives are likely to respond to one another and to make connections between the abstract philosophical concerns about free will and their own lives. I also hope that the book's dialogue format makes it a more pleasant and engaging read.

Freedom, Responsibility, and Determinism

List of Characters

Main Characters:

John, a student

Kate, a student

Professor James Goldfarb, a philosophy teacher

Professor Hugh Daniels, a philosophy teacher

Professor William Ryan, a philosophy teacher

Professor Marcia Gonzalez, a psychology teacher

Reverend Marie Donagan, a college chaplain

Lesser Characters:

Dean Crawford, dean of students

Brian, a student

Rebecca, a student

Armando, a student

Jenny, a student

Janet Richardson, a student

Act 1: The Dilemma of Determinism

Scene 1

Tuesday, 11 a.m. John is walking in the halls of a building that houses both administrative offices and classrooms. He encounters his friend Kate in the hallway.

KATE: Hey, handsome, I'm on my way to Hickok Lab. Wanna carry my books for me?

JOHN: Kate, I'm surprised at you. Here you are a member of the campus' leading feminist organization and you want me to carry your books?

KATE: I thought you would relish the opportunity to exhibit some old-fashioned chivalry.

JOHN: You would actually encourage such behavior?

KATE: What can I say? These books are heavy, and I'm tired of carrying them. I support chivalry that serves my interests.

JOHN: Shameless, but I would oblige. However, I've got a meeting with Dean Crawford.

KATE: What's up?

JOHN: Don't know. Probably judicial board matters.

KATE: Too bad. You could have scored some points by helping me out here.

JOHN: Pub tonight?

KATE: Sure, what time?

JOHN: Nine p.m.? I've gotta hit the books for a while before that.

KATE: Great! See you then.

Kate exits. John heads into Dean Crawford's office, and the secretary motions him to head in to see the dean. John knocks on his open office door.

DEAN CRAWFORD: Hi, John! Come on in.

JOHN: Hi, Dean Crawford. I got your message. What's up?

DEAN CRAWFORD: We've got a case for the student judicial board. As the head of the J-board, you'll need to get a hold of the other members.
  I've got packets with relevant information about the case for each member of the board. Please see to it that each of the other members get theirs.

Dean Crawford hands three large, sealed envelopes to John.

JOHN: What are we looking at here?

DEAN CRAWFORD: It's a plagiarism case. It looks pretty obvious and pretty egregious. But the student wanted her case heard by the J-board.

JOHN: Who is the student?

DEAN CRAWFORD: Janet Richardson. Do you know her?

JOHN: I know of her, but I don't know her personally. I'm shocked though. She's in her third year, and I hear she's a solid student.

DEAN CRAWFORD: That makes two of us.

It's a shame, because if she's found guilty, this could have very serious consequences.

JOHN: I'll say. She could be expelled from school.

DEAN CRAWFORD: Well, get those packets to the other members of the J-board, and our office will set up a hearing with Janet for later in the week.

Also, as usual, keep all matters pertaining to the case strictly confidential.

JOHN: Okay. See you, Dr. Crawford.

John exits. Dean Crawford remains in his office and gets back to work.

Scene 2

Tuesday, 9:30 p.m. John and Kate are seated in a booth enjoying a few beers at a pub in the student center on campus. They see Prof. James Goldfarb, one of their philosophy teachers, enter the pub, and they invite him over to join them. Prof. Goldfarb is happy to do so.

KATE: Hi Professor Goldfarb! Glad you could join us.

JOHN: Yes, would you like a beer?

PROF. GOLDFARB: Sure, I don't see why not.

John heads to the bar to get another mug. Kate and Prof. Goldfarb remain seated.

KATE: John and I were just talking about that murder case from down in Winchester.

PROF. GOLDFARB: Oh, yes, a horrible crime. Such a brutal murder.

KATE: I'll say. The latest news is that the authorities now have very convincing evidence that a man named Christopher Braddock killed both Ken and Marjorie Douglas by bludgeoning them to death with a baseball bat. He then proceeded to remove all kinds of valuables from the house and any money he could find. Braddock was apprehended down in Texas a few days after the bodies were found in the Douglas home.

John returns and pours Prof. Goldfarb a beer.

PROF. GOLDFARB: Thanks, John. Cheers!

JOHN: Say, did you tell Professor Goldfarb what we were discussing?

KATE: Yes, but not what we were debating.

PROF. GOLDFARB: A debate? Do tell. You know how we philosophers love a good debate.

KATE: Well, John thinks that if Christopher Braddock committed this crime he should get the death penalty, and I think that even if he committed it he shouldn't get the death penalty. As you know, I take my Christian beliefs very seriously. And while I know not all Christians share my view, I just don't think that putting a man to death is justified no matter what crime he committed. It seems to me that we all have a capacity for redemption that needs to be respected. Consequently, I'm opposed to the death penalty as a matter of principle.

PROF. GOLDFARB: Hmm, yes, I see. And what about you, John?

JOHN: As I see it, those who freely engage in wrongfully harming others should be made to suffer in an equal proportion to the wrongful harm they have caused. Justice requires that punishment should fit the crime in this way. Thus, assuming that this Christopher Braddock did of his own free will commit the murders of Ken and Marjorie Douglas, I think he should be subjected to the death penalty.

PROF. GOLDFARB: An eye for an eye, eh?

JOHN: Yes, I suppose that's what I'm getting at here.

PROF. GOLDFARB: John, does it matter to you whether the punishment has any deterrent effect? In other words, does it matter to you in any way whether the punishment helps to discourage the criminal and/or others from committing crimes in the future? For instance, suppose that you were part of an island community and you were a prison guard there. Suppose the island was sinking and everyone had fled the island except for you and a man who had been convicted of murder and sentenced to death. Suppose that the island stops sinking just before you are ready to leave so that the island can no longer serve the needs of a larger community but one or two people could survive on the island. Should the murderer be put to death before you leave the island, or should he be left there to live on his own?

JOHN: The way I see it this murderer deserves to die, and failure to put him to death would be a failure to see that justice is done. So, yes, I think this man should be put to death even though putting him to death would not serve in any way the purposes of deterrence.

PROF. GOLDFARB: Ah, so yours is a purely retributive view of punishment. That is, you see punishment as justified solely on the grounds that justice demands that those who have harmed others through their crimes deserve to suffer for what they have done and that the tendency of the punishment or threat of punishment to discourage future crimes is irrelevant to the justification of punishment.

JOHN: Yes, I suppose that is my view.

PROF. GOLDFARB: Hmmm . . .

JOHN: What?

PROF. GOLDFARB: This strikes me as poor grounds upon which to justify punishment.

JOHN: Why?

PROF. GOLDFARB: Because the retributive theory is based on the assumption that people are morally responsible for their decisions and actions in such a way as to make them deserving of punishment for the wrongful harms they have caused to others.

JOHN: I hardly find this assumption to be problematic. People have free will, and because of this they are morally responsible for much of what they do, including many of the wrongful harms they cause to others. Assuming Christopher Braddock acted of his own free will in killing Ken and Marjorie Douglas, he deserves to die for what he has done.

PROF. GOLDFARB: John, what does it mean to say a person acts of his own free will?

JOHN: A person acts freely when his acts are a product of his own choice, and in choosing the agent must have been able to do otherwise. There must have been alternative courses of action he could have chosen to take.

PROF. GOLDFARB: So this means that if Chris Braddock acted of his own free will, then he must have made the choice to commit these murders, and in choosing, he must have been able to do otherwise, that is, he must have been able to have made a different choice.

JOHN: Yes, that's right.

PROF. GOLDFARB: Kate, what do you think about this?

KATE: I have mixed feelings. I agree that we have free will and that to act freely our actions must in some way be a product of choices made in situations where we could have done otherwise. But I think many people can rightly be said to act of their own free will and to be responsible for acting in many cases where their actions are necessitated by their beliefs and desires—you know, in cases where their actions are determined by their character.

Even if Braddock could not have chosen other than to kill the Douglases due to his bad moral character, he still might be said to have freely committed the killings and he still might be morally responsible for the killings.

JOHN: How so?

KATE: Even if his character determined his decision, Braddock could be said to have acted freely and be morally responsible for his action if his character is a product of past decisions he has made in which he could have done otherwise. I do believe that many of the decisions we make are not determined. Many of our decisions are made in contexts in which we really could do otherwise. But I also believe that a lot of what we do is necessitated—determined—by our character. I also think that a lot of these undetermined decisions that we make during our lifetimes help to shape our character, so that when we are determined to act by our character in later life, these earlier undetermined free decisions allow that these later determined decisions are also free and we are responsible for them.

JOHN: I think I see what you're getting at. You're saying that even if Braddock was necessitated by his character to commit the murders, he may still be said to act freely in this case if his character was shaped by past decisions he made that were not necessitated and in which he freely chose to act and could have chosen otherwise. The idea here is that if he freely made himself into the murdering sort that he is, then he may still be rightly said to act freely for murders committed now and he may consequently be rightly said to be responsible for the murders.

    Is this your view?

KATE: Yes.

JOHN: Can we say that determined decisions that issue from the necessitating influences of character have a derivative freedom insofar as they are the product of a character that was formed by past free choices in which the agent could have done otherwise?

KATE: Yes.

JOHN: And because these determined decisions or actions have such a derivative freedom the agents who perform them are thereby responsible for them?

KATE: Yes.

JOHN: I like this view very much, and I embrace it. According to this view, it follows that even if Braddock was causally determined to commit the murders because of his bad moral character we can still rightly view him as having freely committed the murders if he shaped his character by past free decisions he made in contexts where he could have done otherwise. Thus, supposing his actions were determined by his bad character, it would still be right to hold him responsible and deserving of punishment if he had forged his character through free decisions he made in the past. Since it is likely that he did freely forge his character, it is likely he is responsible for the murders and, thus, deserving of a death penalty. Right, Kate?

KATE: Well, maybe. I agree that you have correctly explained how Braddock could be responsible for his actions, but as I said earlier, I'm uncomfortable with the death penalty.

JOHN: Professor Goldfarb, what do you think about this?

PROF. GOLDFARB: Well, while I agree with your account of what free will requires—namely that at least some of our choices be undetermined in such a way that we could have chosen differently—I just don't think that any of our acts meet these requirements. Thus, I don't think anyone is morally responsible or deserving of punishment.

JOHN: What? Are you telling us you're a hard determinist?

PROF. GOLDFARB: Well, if I understand what you mean by **determinism** and **hard determinism**, then, no, I'm not a hard determinist. By the way, what exactly *do* you mean by these terms?

JOHN: Well, as Dr. Ryan told us in our metaphysics course, determinism is the view that at any time the universe has exactly one physically possible future. That is, something is deterministic if it has exactly one physically possible outcome. So, for instance, the determinist would say that even if Braddock chose to murder the Douglases, the choice itself was necessitated as well as all the events leading up to the choice. The determinist might say his choice was determined by neurological events occurring in his brain right before the choice and those events were determined by earlier events and so on going back in time. In this way, we might view his decision as a consequence of genetic and environmental factors beyond his control, which ultimately determined his brain functioning and his choice to commit the murders.

PROF. GOLDFARB: Okay, and **hard determinism** says?

JOHN: Well, hard determinism is simply the view that determinism is true and *because* of this there is no free will.

PROF. GOLDFARB: That's what I thought you meant, but I just wanted to make sure.

JOHN: And . . . are you a hard determinist?

PROF. GOLDFARB: No, I'm not.

JOHN: But you just said you agreed with my account of free will while also asserting that no human actions meet the requirements of free will.

PROF. GOLDFARB: Yes, but I didn't say this *because* I think determinism is true. Hard determinists deny the existence of free will on the grounds that determinism is true. But that's not why *I* deny the existence of free will.

JOHN: Really? What is your view then? But wait, let me get us another pitcher of beer.

John leaves the table to get a refill at the bar.

PROF. GOLDFARB: Kate, shouldn't you guys be working on papers or studying for exams?

KATE: I suppose, but neither of us has any papers due until late next week. Why do today what can be done tomorrow?

PROF. GOLDFARB: I'm a bit of a procrastinator myself.

John returns with a full pitcher and pours another round.

JOHN: Cheers! Now, please explain yourself, Professor Goldfarb.

PROF. GOLDFARB: Well, like I said, hard determinists deny the existence of free will because they think determinism is true. But I don't think determinism is true. Recall that according to determinism *all* events are determined so that at each moment in time there is but one physically possible future. This strikes me and very many others as incompatible with what contemporary physics tells us. According to quantum physics, there are subatomic particles that act in a causally undetermined fashion. This view is somewhat controversial. There are some deterministic ways of understanding quantum physics, but most physicists today think quantum physics is inconsistent with a deterministic worldview. I tend to agree with the latter. But regardless of whether determinism is true or not, we have good reason to believe there is no free will.

JOHN: But the truth or falsity of determinism seems fundamental here. If determinism is false, then doesn't this leave room for the freedom of choice and alternative possibilities that allow for free will?

PROF. GOLDFARB: I doubt it. But we're getting ahead of ourselves. Let me explain further.

KATE AND JOHN: Please do.

PROF. GOLDFARB: My own view is **hard incompatibilism**. **Incompatibilism** is the view that free will is incompatible with the world being deterministic. Hard incompatibilists accept incompatibilism while also maintaining that there is no free will.

Kate and John give Prof. Goldfarb a puzzled look.

PROF. GOLDFARB: Look, the basic idea behind hard incompatibilism is that there is no free will regardless of whether the world is deterministic or not. If the world is deterministic, then there is no free will because determinism rules out the alternative possibilities required for free will. And if there is some indeterminism in the world allowing for some undetermined human decisions and actions, then this does nothing to help establish free will. In fact, indeterminism in human choice and action only makes the prospects for human freedom worse.

JOHN: I see. So you think those who believe in free will are caught on the horns of a dilemma in which neither option supports their case.

PROF. GOLDFARB: Yes, it's called "the dilemma of determinism."

JOHN: Well, I can see why someone would say that if determinism is true, then there is no free will. As I said earlier, free will requires that at least some human choices are made in contexts where we really could make different decisions and act differently. Were determinism true, all of our choices would be necessitated by earlier events so that we couldn't really do or choose otherwise. But I'm really puzzled as to why you say indeterminism does nothing to help establish free will.

PROF. GOLDFARB: What do you find confusing about this?

JOHN: It seems to me that if there was the right kind of indeterminism in the universe, then this *would* help allow for human freedom.

PROF. GOLDFARB: How so?

JOHN: Suppose that some human decisions were causally undetermined. If so, then these decisions would not be necessitated by earlier events. And if they were not necessitated by earlier events, then this means that in making such decisions we really could have done otherwise. Such decisions would be free decisions.

PROF. GOLDFARB: John, I thought you would say something like that. It's a common reaction to the dilemma of determinism. But that line of reasoning doesn't work.

JOHN: Why not?

KATE: Yeah, why not?

PROF. GOLDFARB: To say human freedom requires that some of our decisions are undetermined in this way runs us right into the problem of luck.

JOHN: What are you getting at here?

PROF. GOLDFARB: Consider this. Imagine it's a Thursday night and you have an exam on Friday morning. You believe you should study for the exam, and you start packing up your materials to bring to the library. But then suppose your buddies stop by your room and invite you to a party and you very much want to join them.

KATE: Right, so he needs to make a decision in this context and he's torn as to which of the two options to choose.

PROF. GOLDFARB: Exactly! But now suppose he decides to go and study, and this decision is completely undetermined so that he really could have chosen to go to the party instead.

JOHN: Sounds like the paradigm case of a free decision to me. And a noble one as well, I might add. If only I could make the right decisions more often.

PROF. GOLDFARB: Well, not so fast here. If the decision is undetermined this means that even if everything about your mental states in the moments leading up to the choice were the same then you could have chosen differently.

JOHN: Yeah, so? Is there a problem with this?

PROF. GOLDFARB: Yes, I think so. Let's suppose there would be something wrong with you shirking your responsibilities as a student, so that the moral choice would be to study. Now, we said that if your choice was undetermined, then everything about your mental states in the moments leading up to the choice could have been the same and you could have chosen differently.

JOHN: Yes.

PROF. GOLDFARB: Well, if your choice in this context was a free one, then you should be morally responsible for it, right?

JOHN: Yes.

PROF. GOLDFARB: Now imagine that in some other logically possible world there is someone just like you in all respects, living a life similar in all respects to yours. Let's call him Twin Earth John. And suppose Twin Earth John faces the very same choice—go to the party or go study—and his choice is undetermined. Twin Earth John will be just like you, having all the same mental states you have in the moments leading up to the choice. Finally, suppose that unlike you he chooses to go to the party.

JOHN: Yes, I have to admit to this sort of possibility, but so what? What are you getting at?

KATE: Oh, John, I think you've been caught in a trap here.

PROF. GOLDFARB: Indeed, he has. But it's not just John; it's anyone who holds a theory of freedom such as the one he holds.

JOHN: I don't get it. Will one of you clue me in?

KATE: John, if you and Twin Earth John are exactly the same in the moments leading up to the choice, having all of the same mental states, and you choose differently, then the ultimate choice made is just a matter of luck. And to say that the respective choices of you and Twin Earth John are just matters of luck is to suggest that you and Twin Earth John don't really have control over the decision that gets made.

JOHN: Uh-oh. Continue, but I don't like where this is going.

KATE: Well, if everything about you and Twin Earth John is the same in the moments leading up to the choice and you each make different choices, then there's really nothing about either of you that explains your choices. In this sense, you don't really have control over your choices. So the choices are not products of your will, and you're not responsible for your choices. Right, Professor Goldfarb?

PROF. GOLDFARB: I could not have said it better myself. But I would add that here we're working with a randomly chosen example. However, we can legitimately universalize the point to be that *any* causally undetermined decision would face the same problem, meaning that any such decision cannot rightly be viewed as a free-willed decision.

JOHN: Man, this dilemma of determinism really *is* a problem then. I was certain that there was a way out of at least one of its horns.

PROF. GOLDFARB: You and a lot of others have thought there is a way out of it. At this point, I'm pretty much convinced there's no way out. That's why I believe there is no free will. There's no room for it in our universe whether everything is determined or whether there is some indeterminism.

JOHN: Dr. Goldfarb, if there's no free will, then do you also think people are not responsible for their decisions and actions?

PROF. GOLDFARB: Yes, that's my view.

JOHN: Well, then assuming Braddock committed those murders, what do you think should be done with him? Should he be punished even though he's not responsible for committing the murders?

PROF. GOLDFARB: That's an interesting question. Recall that earlier I said the retributive theory of punishment, which you endorse, is problematic.

JOHN: Yes, on my view criminals should be punished for their wrongful behavior simply because they deserve to suffer for the harms they have caused.

PROF. GOLDFARB: Right, but as I've shown, people lack free will and so they are not responsible for their decisions and actions. Thus, no one really *deserves* anything—neither rewards nor punishments. But this just shows the retributive theory of punishment is problematic. Punishment could still quite possibly be justified on the grounds of deterrence.

JOHN: You mean criminals like Braddock could still be punished to prevent them from committing more crimes in the future and to serve as an example to others, threatening them to conform to the laws. Having a penal system and punishing offenders is also justified on the grounds of providing a disincentive to the general public, discouraging them from engaging in criminal activity.

PROF. GOLDFARB: Exactly.

JOHN: Well, I'm glad we can at least agree that punishments should still be administered. I shudder to think about the chaos that would likely occur were there no penal system.

KATE: Wait a minute. What about the death penalty? John, you were arguing that Braddock should be put to death on the grounds that he deserves to die for killing the Douglases.

JOHN: Yes, I did make this argument. If Professor Goldfarb is right, then Braddock doesn't *deserve* to die. But I suppose he should still be put to death even if he's not responsible, because the death penalty provides such a strong deterrent to murder—one of the most awful crimes. Right, Dr. Goldfarb?

PROF. GOLDFARB: I'm afraid not, John.

JOHN: What? Really? But surely awful crimes like murder deserve a very strong deterrent. What could be stronger than the threat of death?

PROF. GOLDFARB: Well, a lot of things could be stronger than the threat of death. If we punished murderers with three years of torture followed by death that would probably provide some additional deterrent effect, but should we do this?

JOHN: No.

PROF. GOLDFARB: Whew! I'm glad we can agree on that. But it's beside the point. Ultimately, I don't think deterrence provides a sound basis for the death penalty, because there's just too much sociological data that shows that the death penalty has no greater deterrent effect at reducing murder rates than does incarceration. Furthermore, it costs the state a lot more money to put a man to death than it does to imprison him, because of all the legal hoops through which it must maneuver. So I'm opposed to the death penalty, and no, I don't think Braddock should be put to death.

JOHN: Gosh, Professor Goldfarb. You must think my views on punishment are pretty primitive.

PROF. GOLDFARB: "The Death Penalty! So easy to endorse even a caveman can do it!"

All three laugh.

PROF. GOLDFARB: Kidding aside, I don't think that at all. One of the greatest minds in the history of philosophy was a staunch advocate of the death penalty. So you're in good company.

JOHN: Who? Genghis Khan?

PROF. GOLDFARB: Ha! He doesn't come to mind when I consider great thinkers. I was thinking of Immanuel Kant.

JOHN: I'm feeling better. That's good company to be in.

KATE: Professor Goldfarb, there's something that troubles me about your deterrence theory of punishment. I'm especially worried about how you combine it with your belief that human beings lack free will and moral responsibility for their actions.

PROF. GOLDFARB: Yes, what's your worry?

KATE: Well, if the sole purpose and/or justification for punishing is deterrence, then why should we only punish the guilty—those who have actually committed crimes? Punishing the innocent while treating them as if they were guilty would serve the purposes of deterrence just as well. Suppose authorities didn't know who killed the Douglases, but they decided to frame an innocent man so as to discourage crime in the community. This could be an effective strategy of deterrence.

PROF. GOLDFARB: Hmm . . . yes, I see. But you also mentioned something about there being a problem with my combining the deterrence theory with the view that there is no free will.

KATE: Yes. You see, one way to solve the problem I've presented is to combine the deterrence theory with some elements of the retributive theory. We might embrace the deterrence theory in the sense that for punishment to be justified it must have some significant deterrent effect. But we might at the same time regard actual guilt and the corresponding notion of desert as also necessary for justified punishment. This would not be a pure retributive theory since it does not regard desert as sufficient for punishment, but rather, only as necessary. It is not a pure deterrence theory either, since it appeals to the concept of desert in the justification of punishment.

This deterrence theory that I propose includes the retributive requirement that actual guilt is necessary for justified punishment. Such a theory could escape the problem of punishing the innocent.

PROF. GOLDFARB: Yes, some philosophers prefer such a hybrid theory of punishment for the very reasons you've mentioned.

KATE: Right, but you can't reasonably adopt this hybrid theory.

PROF. GOLDFARB: Right, since I deny the existence of free will and moral responsibility, no one is actually guilty of committing crimes or deserving of punishment for committing them. Thus, I cannot regard the desert of the criminal as a necessary condition for punishment. Thus, the hybrid theory is not an option for hard incompatibilists like me. Right?

KATE: Yep. And so you're stuck with the pure deterrence theory of punishment and this problem regarding the punishment of the innocent.

PROF. GOLDFARB: I must say, Kate, that's a well-made point. John, you're lucky to have such a smart girl to hang around with.

JOHN: If she's so smart, why's she hanging around with me?

KATE: That's what I keep asking myself.

JOHN: I like smart women. I'll have to find one to marry someday.

KATE: Better develop your mind then.

JOHN: Yes, maybe. But let's get back to the argument. Professor Goldfarb, what's your response?

PROF. GOLDFARB: If you insist. As a pure deterrence theorist, my answer to the problem of punishing the innocent is simply that as a matter of fact our society has a strong sense of justice, which includes a belief that innocent people should not be punished for crimes they did not commit. This widespread sentiment should be respected so as to avoid the public outrage that would occur if it were discovered that innocent people were being punished for crimes.

I also believe that there is substantial benefit to the citizens in feeling secure in their persons. Society is a happier place when citizens can rest assured that innocent citizens will not intentionally be singled out by the government and subjected to punishments for crimes they did not commit. Thus, as I see it, even a pure deterrence theorist has good reasons to reject the practice of punishing the innocent.

KATE: Those are good points, but I'm still a bit concerned that there's no principled argument here against punishing the innocent. It still seems to me that on the pure deterrence theory if you could be absolutely certain that by punishing an innocent man crime would be reduced and that no one would ever find out that an innocent man was being punished, then the pure deterrence theory would provide no grounds for refusing to punish the innocent in such a case.

PROF. GOLDFARB: Yes, but those conditions are never met. We cannot have certainty about these things. So even on the pure deterrence theory the punishing of the innocent is never justified.

KATE: I suppose, but I'm still uncomfortable with it.

Prof. Goldfarb, John, and Kate all remain silent for a while. They sit still in their thoughts, sipping the last of their beers.

JOHN (*suddenly*): Professor Goldfarb, I feel quite bad about myself from time to time when I shirk my duties as a student or when I don't treat others as well as I think I should. Maybe one benefit of adopting your view would be that it might give me some relief from these feelings of guilt and inadequacy. I mean, if I lack free will, then I'm not really responsible for these inadequacies in my character and conduct.

PROF. GOLDFARB: Yes, this is a potential benefit of adopting hard incompatibilism. It can help us be kinder and gentler to ourselves. Not only that, it can also help us be kinder and gentler to others, and it can help us overcome the resentments that we often feel toward others when they do not act in the ways we believe they should.

A lot of human misery stems from our own feelings of personal guilt and the resentment we feel toward others. Recognition that we lack free will and moral responsibility can help us overcome the damaging effects of these emotions.

Silence overcomes the trio once again.

KATE: You know, regarding these latter points about how hard incompatibilism can help us overcome guilt and resentment, this point seems like a double-edged sword. This aspect of hard incompatibilism also seems to encourage moral backsliding. You know, going on moral holiday. If I'm not morally responsible for what I do, then why should I care that much about acting wrongly if I see that I can get away with it?

PROF. GOLDFARB: Another good point, Kate. This kind of consideration has led some who believe there is no free will to say that we should continue to foster the illusion of free will. Saul Smilansky makes this point in his book *Free Will and Illusion*. He doesn't think we should actively deceive people into believing in free will by spreading misinformation. Rather, he thinks most people already believe we have free will, and since this widespread belief in free will is good for society, he thinks we should not undermine belief in it by espousing free will skepticism. Personally I'm not sure what I want to say about this.

I suspect that there would not be a lot of moral backsliding if hard incompatibilism were widely accepted. Society imposes a lot of moral expectations on us. We are expected to be law abiding and decent, and it's in each of our self-interests to live in a community where this is expected of us. Even if hard incompatibilism were widely accepted there would still be good reason for each of us to want the moral norms upheld, and we would for the most part conform to these norms due to the effects of social conditioning.

KATE: I don't know. I'm still skeptical.

Silence falls over the trio again. Prof. Goldfarb checks his watch.

PROF. GOLDFARB: Well, it's getting late, and I've still got some papers to grade. Thanks for the beer and even more thanks for the stimulating conversation. See you.

Prof. Goldfarb leaves.

JOHN: Well, speaking of moral backsliding, would you care to join me for some guilt-free partying at the Beta house?

KATE: John, you're incorrigible.

JOHN: I can't help myself.

KATE: No thanks. I'm going to go study.

Study Questions

1. Define determinism, hard determinism, and hard incompatibilism. Make clear the differences between them.

2. What findings in contemporary physics present a significant threat to the truth of determinism?

3. Explain the dilemma of determinism, making clear how this supports hard incompatibilism.

4. Explain the problem of luck that confronts those who believe free-willed acts must be causally undetermined.

5. Explain the difference between the retributive theory of punishment and the deterrence theory of punishment.

6. Explain why hard incompatibilism presents a challenge to the retributive theory of punishment.

7. Explain the problem of punishing the innocent. For which theory of punishment is this a problem?

8. What points about guilt and resentment are made in support of hard incompatibilism? Explain how these points might be viewed as a double-edged sword.

Discussion Questions

1. Does the dilemma of determinism show there is no free will? Consider some possible objections to this argument. Can the objections be reasonably answered?

2. Those who believe free-willed acts must be causally undetermined are faced with the problem of luck. Is there no way out of this problem? Consider some possible responses to this problem. Are your responses adequate?

3. Do considerations about guilt and resentment make hard incompatibilism more attractive or less attractive? Explain your answer.

4. Of the three theories of punishment considered in this act—the pure retributive theory, the pure deterrence theory, or the mixed theory—which seems the most plausible? Explain.

Suggestions for Further Reading

Act 1 presents us with theories of free will and theories of punishment. Regarding free will, this act focuses on the view that there is no free will. We are introduced to both hard determinism and hard incompatibilism. We might describe these theories as two kinds of free will skepticism. For a good survey of such skeptical theories, see Robert Kane's *A Contemporary Introduction to Free Will* (2005), Ch. 7. Two famous defenders of hard determinism are Baron Paul d'Holbach (1770) and Paul Edwards (1958). An excerpt from Baron d'Holbach's writing revealing his hard determinist views can be found in Joel Feinberg and Russ Shafer-Landau's *Reason and Responsibility*, 10th ed. (1999), pp. 416–21. Paul Edwards' essay can be found in Robert Kane's *Free Will* (2002b), pp. 59–67. As noted in Act 1, most free will skeptics these days favor hard incompatibilism, since it would seem that contemporary physics undermines determinism. For defenses of hard incompatibilism, see Ted Honderich (1993), Derk Pereboom (2001, 2007), Saul Smilansky (2000), and Galen Strawson (1986). In Act 1, the view that hard incompatibilism is true but we should preserve the illusion of free will is mentioned. This view is defended in Smilansky (2000).

The luck argument has been given a lot of attention in the recent literature. The version of the argument presented in Act 1 is derived from Alfred Mele (1999a,b). His is perhaps the most cited version of the argument. For other defenses of the luck argument, see Mark Bernstein (1995), Bernard Berofsky (2000), Randolph Clarke (1995, 2002), John M. Fischer (1999), Ishtiyaque Haji (1999), Timothy O'Connor (2000), Galen Strawson (2000), Peter van Inwagen (2002), and Bruce Waller (1988).

The conception of free-willed action developed in Act 1 is an incompatibilist conception of free will. Here belief in the existence of free will is understood as incompatible with determinism—the belief that all events are necessitated in such a way that at any time there is only one physically possible future. The view put forth in Act 1 allows that some of our free acts may be determined by our character, but for those to be free we must have freely constructed our character through previous free choices that were not causally determined. This view has its roots in the views of Aristotle (see *Nicomachean Ethics*, Bk. III, 1925). Aristotle believed we could be responsible for acts necessitated by our character as long as our character is a product of our free choice. However, it is not clear that Aristotle believed the free choice of our character required any indeterminacy in our decision making. For a contemporary defense of this sort of view, developed clearly along incompatibilist lines, see Robert Kane (1996, 2007). The relevant portions of Aristotle's *Nicomachean Ethics*, Bk. III can be found in Pereboom's *Free Will* (2009). Pereboom's book is a collection of writings on the subject, which includes historically important works and some important recent and contemporary pieces.

Regarding the theories of punishment, we are introduced to both pure retributivism and the pure deterrence theory. There is also some discussion of a hybrid view, which combines elements of retributivism and the deterrence view. For a good introduction to the main theories of punishment and the arguments for and against them, see Martin Golding's *Philosophy of Law* (1975), Ch. 4 and 5 in particular. Another introduction to the issues is Joel Feinberg's "The Classic Debate," which can be found in Feinberg and Coleman's *Philosophy of Law*, 6th ed. (2000). The Feinberg and Coleman book contains other good essays on punishment; see especially Michael Moore's defense of retributivism (1987) and Russ Schafer-Landau's critique of it (1996). For a more extensive collection of writings on the subject of punishment, see Michael Gorr and Sterling Harwood's *Crime and Punishment: Philosophic Explorations* (1995). This collection contains writings defending each of the three views of punishment considered in Act 1—pure retributivism, pure deterrence theory, and the mixed view. It also contains discussions of other theories of punishment, such as the rehabilitation and the restitution theories.

The most famous historical source on the pure deterrence theory is probably Jeremy Bentham; see his *An Introduction to the Principles of Morals and Legislation* (1970). Gorr and Harwood's *Crime and Punishment* contains a nice excerpt from this classic work by Bentham. Perhaps the most famous historical source on the retributive theory of punishment is Immanuel Kant; see his *The Philosophy of Law, Part II* (1887). An excerpt from this work is included in James White's *Contemporary Moral Problems*, 10th edition (2012). This excerpt reveals the nature of his retributive theory and his case for the death penalty. It even includes an example very similar to the example of the sinking island that is considered in Act 1. James White's book contains other works on the subject of the death penalty by more recent and contemporary thinkers, such as Ernest Van Den Haag (1986) and Jeffrey Reiman (1998). For other notable work on the death penalty, see Hugo Bedau (1991) and Anthony Amsterdam (1977).

Act 2: Compatibilism

Scene 1

Wednesday, 3 p.m. John and Kate are in the philosophy department lounge with Prof. Daniels, telling him about their conversation with Prof. Goldfarb from the previous night.

Prof. Goldfarb enters and pours himself a cup of coffee.

PROF. DANIELS (*jokingly*): I hear you've been spreading this hard incompatibilist tripe to our students again.

PROF. GOLDFARB: Yes, "corrupting their minds" is what some would call it.

PROF. DANIELS: Ha! Yes! It's a dirty job, but that's what they pay us for.
　Say, I hope you guys gave some serious consideration to the compatibilist position last night.

PROF. GOLDFARB: No, not really. The conversation just didn't head that direction. I'm glad it didn't. It seems to me that view is just another philosophical dead end.

PROF. DANIELS: I don't think so.

JOHN: Professor Daniels, what's the **compatibilist** view?

PROF. DANIELS: It's the view that human freedom and responsibility are consistent with determinism. That is, even if all events, including human decisions and actions, are necessitated by earlier events, we may still rightly be said to sometimes act of our own free will and sometimes be responsible for our decisions and actions.

JOHN: Wait a minute. Lee me see if I understand this. This morning I thought about staying in bed instead of going to class. Ultimately, I got up and went to class because I really want to bring up my GPA. Are you suggesting that even if everything that occurs in this world is determined, including my decision to go to class this morning, then we could still be acting freely?

PROF. DANIELS: Yes.

JOHN: And in your view even though my decision to go to class may have been causally determined by my beliefs and desires and these may have been determined by my brain functioning and my brain functioning may have been determined by genetic and environmental factors, all of this is consistent with my decision being freely made?

PROF. DANIELS: That's right.

JOHN: I don't see how that can be right.

KATE: Me neither.

PROF. DANIELS (*smiling*): I can see you've really corrupted them this time, Jim.

PROF. GOLDFARB: One man's corruption is another man's enlightenment.

PROF. DANIELS: Tripe by any other name is still tripe.

PROF. GOLDFARB: Well, perhaps you could disabuse us of these ill-conceived notions we've got in our heads.

PROF. DANIELS: Gladly.

PROF. GOLDFARB: Okay, why don't you start by telling us what you mean by "freedom."

PROF. DANIELS Well, how's this? A person is free if and only if he has the power to do what he wants and there are no constraints preventing him from doing as he wants. So for instance, I am in this room with you now because I want to be here and I'm not here as a matter of being threatened to be here nor because I'm chained to this seat. As such, I'm here of my own free will.

PROF. GOLDFARB: Sounds like the classical compatibilism of the sort advocated by Hobbes, Hume, and Mill.

PROF. DANIELS: That's right. It seems like a good place to start our discussion.

JOHN: Professor Daniels, why should we think this kind of freedom is consistent with determinism?

KATE: Yeah, and what considerations should lead us to think this is a correct account of freedom?

PROF. DANIELS: John, consider the example I gave. In the compatibilist view I'm presenting, I'm here simply because, one, I want to be here and, two, I'm not here as a consequence of being threatened or physically forced, such as being chained to my seat. According to this view, whether my desire to be here because I want to be here determines my choice to be here and/ or whether this desire is determined by my brain functioning is irrelevant to the question of my freedom. Thus, this conception of human freedom suggests the existence of it is perfectly consistent with a deterministic universe. Do you see what I'm getting at?

JOHN: Yes, I guess so.

KATE: What about my question? Why should we think your account of freedom is correct?

PROF. DANIELS: Well, look, when we hold people responsible for what they've done and, say, blame them for their decisions or actions, we do so on the assumption that they have acted freely, right?

KATE: Yes.

PROF. DANIELS: And we don't blame people for their actions when the harm they've caused is accidental. For instance, if unbeknownst to me my son has put poison in a cup that I believe to be full of water and I give it to you to drink, then you don't blame me for the harm I've caused, right?

KATE: Right.

PROF. DANIELS: And why not?

KATE: Because in this case you don't want to poison me. You don't do it of your own free will.

PROF. DANIELS: Exactly. Nor would you blame me if I bring harm upon you by external force or coercion. For instance, if someone threatens to kill my child unless I steal $100 from your bank account, then again you don't blame me. In this case, there's a very real sense in which I'm not doing what I want to do.

KATE: Right, you don't want to steal the money; rather, you are forced into doing so by the threat.

PROF. DANIELS: So you see we only hold people responsible when they are doing what they want to do and they are not acting as a result of threat or external physical force.

KATE: Oh, I see, and since we agreed earlier that we only hold people responsible when they act of their own free will, it follows that you've given a correct account of the nature of human freedom.

PROF. DANIELS: Exactly.

JOHN: God bless you, Professor Daniels! Last night, Professor Goldfarb had me convinced there was no free will. But that's because I assumed that free-willed acts had to be causally undetermined. This led into the problem of luck. However, you're arguing free-willed acts don't have to be causally undetermined. We overlooked this possibility last night.

PROF. DANIELS: It's a common mistake.

JOHN: Well, I'm glad you've pointed this out.

PROF. DANIELS: You're welcome.

JOHN: Professor Goldfarb, what do you think about this?

PROF. GOLDFARB (smiling): It's tripe. And Professor Daniels knows he'll have to do better than this.

JOHN AND KATE: How so?

PROF. GOLDFARB: Look, for persons to act freely they have to be able to do otherwise, and there is no way for the determinist to account for this.

PROF. DANIELS: But I think I can account for this.

PROF. GOLDFARB: No, you can't.

PROF. DANIELS: Alright then, why not?

PROF. GOLDFARB: Look, you agree with me that if determinism is true, then our present actions are the necessary consequences of the past and the laws of nature, right? For instance, if determinism is true, then there are certain laws that govern the operation of things in our universe—the sort of natural laws discovered by scientists, such as the universal laws of gravitation and the laws of thermodynamics—and my speaking to you now would just be the necessary consequence of the workings of these laws and the state of affairs just prior to my speaking to you, right?

PROF. DANIELS: Right, presumably just prior to speaking to me your brain was in a certain neurological state that in accord with certain laws of nature necessitated your speaking to me now.

PROF. GOLDFARB: And this is just the example we're working with, right? I mean the point can be universalized to *all* events. We might say my speaking to you now was necessitated by an earlier neurological event in my brain, but that neurological event was itself necessitated by an earlier event, which was in turn necessitated by an earlier event and so on, right?

PROF. DANIELS: Sure, this is all just part of the deterministic understanding of how the universe operates.

PROF. GOLDFARB: Okay, good. So we agree on this. Now, tell me, can we change the past or the laws of nature?

PROF. DANIELS: No, of course not. Regarding the past, what's done is done and we cannot go back in time to change it nor can we change the natural laws—the ones discovered by natural scientists—which govern the way things operate in our universe.

PROF. GOLDFARB: Well, look, if we cannot change the past and the laws of nature and if, according to determinism, what we do now is a necessary consequence of the past and the laws of nature, then, according to determinism, there is nothing we can do now to change the fact that our present actions are the necessary consequences of the past and the laws of nature.

PROF. DANIELS: Yes, so?

PROF. GOLDFARB: Well, if, according to determinism, there is nothing we can do now to change the fact that our present actions are the necessary consequences of the past and the laws of nature, then it ultimately follows that if determinism is true then there is nothing we can do now to change the fact that our present actions occur. But this of course is just to say that if determinism is true then we cannot do otherwise than we actually do.

PROF. DANIELS: Ah, I see. And I suppose your point is also that not only are *we* presently incapable of doing otherwise, but if determinism is true then *no one* can ever do otherwise than what they in fact do, right?

PROF. GOLDFARB: Yep.

PROF. DANIELS: And I suppose you also think human freedom requires a capacity to do otherwise. So that ultimately, and in direct opposition to my own compatibilist view, you are suggesting free will and determinism are *not* compatible.

PROF. GOLDFARB: Precisely.

PROF. DANIELS: Well, I'm familiar with this, this . . . what's the name of this kind of argument?

PROF. GOLDFARB: The "Consequence Argument."

PROF. DANIELS: Yes, well, I'm familiar with this Consequence Argument. And I know of two ways of responding to it, but I certainly favor one approach over the other.

PROF. GOLDFARB: Do tell.

Prof. Daniels is about to respond but he notices that Kate is straining to get back into the conversation.

PROF. DANIELS: Gladly. But wait. What is it, Kate?

KATE: I think I know a way out of this Consequence Argument.

PROF. DANIELS: Okay, shoot.

KATE: In our metaphysics class, Dr. Ryan said that many compatibilists think we *can* do otherwise than what we do even if our acts are causally determined. If that's right, then there has to be something wrong with the Consequence Argument.

PROF. DANIELS: Yes, this is one of the strategies that I had in mind for responding to the Consequence Argument. Personally, I don't like this approach.

KATE: Why not?

PROF. DANIELS: Well, tell me more about what you had in mind. I think I know where you're going with this, but I'm not sure just yet.

KATE: Okay, like I said, many compatibilists believe we could do otherwise even if our acts are causally determined. They provide what's called a **conditional analysis** of "could have done otherwise." So for instance, consider the case of John going to class this morning. He contemplated staying in bed and not going to class, but he got up and went to class.

PROF. DANIELS: Yes, and the compatibilists will say this decision and action were freely performed even if they were causally determined by the neurological states of his brain leading up to the decision and action. Indeed, according to compatibilism such actions may be freely performed even if all events in this universe are causally determined.

KATE: Yes. But as I was saying, many compatibilists think such free acts can be determined and the agent still could do otherwise. The compatibilist may say that the phrase "the agent could have done otherwise" just means "he *would* have done otherwise, *if* he had wanted to or chose to." So for instance, even though John's decision to go to class was causally determined, he still *could* have done otherwise in the sense that he would have done otherwise if he had wanted to.

PROF. DANIELS: Right, the idea here is that John's decision to go to class was determined by his stronger desire to improve his GPA. But, even though the decision was determined, he could have done otherwise in the sense that if he'd had a stronger desire to stay in bed then he would have.

KATE: Yes, and all of this just goes to show that there must be something wrong with the Consequence Argument. For as I've just argued, there's a very real sense in which even though agents are causally determined they still could do otherwise.

JOHN: I wonder what exactly the problem is with the Consequence Argument.

KATE: Yeah, me too. My comments here give grounds for doubting the legitimacy of the argument, but they don't pinpoint precisely where the argument goes wrong.

PROF. DANIELS: Kate, you've certainly done a nice job articulating this line of response to the Consequence Argument, and this *is* the kind of response I thought you had in mind. But as I said earlier, I don't like this kind of response.

KATE: Why not?

JOHN: Yeah, Professor Daniels, why not?

PROF. DANIELS: Because the conditional analysis of "could have done otherwise" is problematic.

JOHN AND KATE: How so?

PROF. DANIELS: I'll use a famous example from the philosophical literature on this subject. Suppose there's a woman named Rosa who as a child was traumatized by a run-in she had with a Labrador retriever, and suppose this experience has rendered her incapable of wanting to touch a blond-haired dog. Now imagine that in her adult life a friend presents her with two puppies to choose from as a pet. The friend tells her to pick up the one she wants. Also, imagine that one of the puppies is a blond Lab and the other is a black Lab.

JOHN: So she picks up the black Lab because she can't bring herself to want to touch the blond Lab.

PROF. DANIELS: Right. But now notice what this tells us about the conditional analysis of "could have done otherwise." Rosa picked up the black Lab, and according to the conditional analysis she could have done otherwise and picked up the blond Lab in the sense that if she had wanted to pick up the blond Lab, then she *would* have.

Now it's true that if she had wanted to pick up the blond Lab, then she would have. But notice this does not mean she could have done so, because as I said earlier she has been rendered psychologically incapable of wanting to touch a blond Lab.

KATE: I get it. The example shows that the conditional analysis of "could have done otherwise" will lead us to say agents could have done otherwise in situations where they really could *not* have done otherwise. Thus, it must be mistaken.

PROF. DANIELS: Precisely, and the case I've presented here is just one of many possible scenarios in which the conditional analysis will lead to the wrong conclusion.

Silence falls over Prof. Daniels, Prof. Goldfarb, Kate, and John momentarily.

PROF. GOLDFARB: Some shrewd logic, Professor Daniels. I might add that as a hard incompatibilist, who believes free will is incompatible with determinism and that free will does not exist, I couldn't agree more. Freedom and moral responsibility require the capacity to do otherwise. And like I said, the Consequence Argument shows why freedom and determinism are incompatible.

PROF. DANIELS: Not so fast my friend. As I said earlier, there are at least two possible ways of responding to the Consequence Argument. We've only considered one of them—the one I don't favor—in which it is argued that there is a plausible compatibilist account of "could have done otherwise." Like you, I don't think this is a good response to the Consequence Argument. However, I would note that in recent years attempts have been made to revise the compatibilist account of "could have done otherwise" so as to avoid the kind of problem I have noted here. I remain skeptical of these attempts, but they might be able to withstand criticism. Regardless, I do think the Consequence Argument can be refuted using a very different strategy.

PROF. GOLDFARB: Yes, go on. What do you have in mind?

PROF. DANIELS: Well, quite simply I reject the view that freedom and responsibility require alternative possibilities—that is, I believe one can act freely even if he could not have done otherwise.

PROF. GOLDFARB: I see. The Consequence Argument assumes that human freedom and responsibility require the capacity to do otherwise. But you think this assumption is false and so the Consequence Argument fails to refute compatibilism. Is that it?

PROF. DANIELS: That's right.

PROF. GOLDFARB: Alright . . . out with it. What's your argument?

JOHN (*to Kate*): This promises to be interesting.

KATE: I'll say.

PROF. DANIELS: Well, one way to make the point would have us consider the following: suppose you offered me a thousand dollars, or even a million dollars, to torture an innocent person. If you did, then I, like many decent people, could not bring myself to do so. My character simply won't allow me to do such a thing.

But notice even though such is the case we don't feel praise for such moral decency is inappropriate. We don't think it inappropriate to say, "Daniels, you acted nobly in refusing to commit such a horrible act." Thus, we rightly view people as responsible when they couldn't do otherwise. Furthermore, since such responsibility presupposes that one has acted of his own free will, it follows that freedom of action does not require a capacity to do otherwise.

PROF. GOLDFARB: Yes, I'm familiar with this line of argument. Daniel Dennett argues along these lines. But I don't buy it.

PROF. DANIELS: Oh? Why not?

PROF. GOLDFARB: Given the way you set up the example it makes sense to praise you for your noble action even though you couldn't do otherwise. But that's because we're only considering you as an adult with a fully formed character. Presumably, there have been situations in your past where you've made choices and where you really could have done otherwise; and presumably, these choices you've made in the past where you could have done otherwise have helped to shape the person you are today.

What I'm suggesting is that you could have formed a different character through past free choices you've made where you could have done otherwise. And this is why we're willing to praise you today for actions you do—such as refusing to torture an innocent man for pay—even though you couldn't do otherwise.

Suppose you *never* could have done otherwise. Suppose that just by the luck of your genetic and environmental background you have, through no efforts of your own, been shaped into the morally decent sort you are who cannot bring himself to torture an innocent person for money. And suppose we know that such is the case. Were this the case we would no longer feel that praising you is called for, because we wouldn't view you as responsible since you played no role in forming this character that now determines your action.

PROF. DANIELS: Hmm . . . these are good points. I see I'm going to have to run the argument at a deeper level.

PROF. GOLDFARB: Well, what do you have in mind? Frankfurt-type examples?

PROF. DANIELS: Well, yes.

JOHN: What are these Frankfurt-type examples?

PROF. DANIELS: These are examples that were originally created by Harry Frankfurt in the late twentieth century. They are designed to show that human freedom and responsibility do not require the capacity to do otherwise—they do not require alternative possibilities.

PROF. GOLDFARB: Yes, and Frankfurt-type examples develop in a more refined way a point that seems to have first been noted by John Locke back in the seventeenth century.

PROF. DANIELS: The recent literature on free will is full of discussions of the Frankfurt-type cases.

JOHN: Do tell. How can they be used to help make the case for compatibilism?

PROF. DANIELS: What I was suggesting is that people can act freely and responsibly even if they can't do otherwise. Thus, even if determinism is true and even if determinism rules out the capacity to do otherwise we can still possess freedom and responsibility.

JOHN: Right, and the example you employed from Daniel Dennett was intended to show this, but it didn't seem to work for the reasons cited by Professor Goldfarb.

PROF. DANIELS: Right, but I think Frankfurt-type examples that avoid the kind of problem he raised can be constructed.

JOHN: Yes, go on.

PROF. DANIELS: Well, consider this: imagine that there is a very powerful being who knows at each moment in your life what you are thinking and what you are about to decide whenever you are in situations calling for choice. And imagine that this being can intervene and make you choose differently if at any moment you are going to choose to act in a way that he does not want you to choose. Finally, also imagine that you are entirely ignorant of the existence of this ever-watchful being.

To illustrate, suppose he wants you to vote for a Republican presidential candidate, and imagine he knows your thoughts as you deliberate in the voting booth. If he sees that your deliberations lead to the Republican choice, then he does not intervene and he allows you to go on and vote Republican. But if he sees that your deliberations are leading you toward choosing the Democratic candidate, then he will intervene and get you to vote Republican.

KATE: Interesting. I can see how this might lead to the view that persons can act freely even though they can't do otherwise.

JOHN: How so?

KATE: Well, suppose this scenario really exists, and you go into the voting booth and decide to vote Republican. In this case, the all-powerful intervener doesn't intervene with your conduct in any way. Further, you are just voting in accord with your own wishes and not as a matter of threat or physical force. Thus, your choice is freely made.

JOHN: Ah, I see. But at the same time that it's freely made I couldn't do otherwise, because if I were to start deliberating in the direction of some other candidate the intervener would step in and exert control over my choice.

KATE: Yes. Isn't this right, Professor Daniels?

PROF. DANIELS: Absolutely.

PROF. GOLDFARB: Well, that's all fine and good, but I don't see how it solves the kind of problem I raised earlier. Suppose John votes Republican in this case because that's just the kind of person he is, and suppose he has not chosen to be this sort of person in contexts where he could have done otherwise. If this were the case, I don't see that his choice to vote Republican is a free act.

PROF. DANIELS: Ah, but notice I had us imagine that the intervener is watching John and reading his thoughts throughout his entire life. Again, imagine that the intervener can and will intervene at any point when John is not going to choose or act as the intervener wants him to.

Now suppose John just happens to always do and think and deliberate in precisely the ways the intervener wants him to so that he never has to intervene in any of John's decisions. In this situation, John will have lived his life in accord with his own plan and decisions and his character will have been a product of his own choices, but he never could have chosen otherwise because if he were to begin to do so the intervener would have detected that he was about to do so and intervened, prohibiting any such choice. It seems to me that in this scenario John has exhibited as much freedom in living his life and has as much responsibility for his choices as anyone could hope to have, but he never could have done otherwise due to the presence of the ever-watchful being who unbeknownst to John is watching and might intervene at any moment.

PROF. GOLDFARB: These considerations do run deep. I see now that this presents us with a scenario where the agent never could have done otherwise, but his actions often result from his own deliberative processes, and his deliberate choices in the past have shaped the character he has today. Thus, he does *seem* to act freely and responsibly even though he can't do otherwise.

I don't know what I want to say about this. But here comes Bill Ryan! Maybe he can take up the argument in my stead.

Prof. William Ryan, another philosophy teacher, has been listening in on the conversation while getting himself a snack and some coffee.

PROF. RYAN: Hi, gentlemen, John, Kate.

PROF. GOLDFARB: Folks, I've got to go. My term papers won't grade themselves. I wish I could stay.

Bill, did you hear the scenario that Professor Daniels constructed with the ever-watchful intervener?

PROF. RYAN (*smiling*): Yes, I did. It's the typical wretched subterfuge one would expect from a compatibilist.

PROF. GOLDFARB: Well, I know you and I disagree on the free will issue but at least we are in agreement about compatibilism. Will you take up the argument for me in my absence?

PROF. RYAN: Yes, but will I be paid?

PROF. GOLDFARB: A penny for your thoughts.

PROF. RYAN: Ha! Well, what else is new. John, Kate, don't go into philosophy if you want to be rich.

PROFS. DANIELS AND RYAN: Bye, Jim.

Professor Goldfarb exits.

PROF. DANIELS: Well, you heard the argument. Any thoughts?

PROF. RYAN: Yes. First of all, I would note that many people believe free-willed decisions must be causally undetermined right up to the moment of choice. Second, those who believe this have no reason to find your argument convincing.

PROF. DANIELS: Oh, and why is this?

PROF. RYAN: Let's go back to the example you gave with John deliberating in the voting booth as to whether he should vote Republican or Democrat.

PROF. DANIELS: Yes, okay.

PROF. RYAN: Well, many folks believe that if his choice is freely made, then it must be causally undetermined right up to the moment of choice. But if the decision is causally undetermined in this way, then the ever-watchful intervener won't be able to know what his choice will be until he actually makes it. If so, then the intervener won't be able to intervene and prevent the choice if John chooses to vote Democratic contrary to his wishes. Perhaps, in this case, whichever way John chooses John will choose freely and be responsible for his choice, but then he also could have done otherwise since the choice was causally undetermined.

Furthermore, suppose while John deliberates the ever-watchful intervener says to himself, "Damn, I can't tell what John's going to do; I think I will preemptively intervene and guide his deliberation in the direction of the Republican candidate." Suppose he does this. Then John's choice will be causally determined and he will not have been able to do otherwise, but the choice will not be freely made nor will John be responsible for it since the intervener will have taken control of the deliberation process himself, removing it from John's control.

PROF. DANIELS: Ah, I think I see. Your point is that those who believe free decisions are causally undetermined have no reason to accept Frankfurt-type examples as evidence that free will and responsibility do not require the agent's capacity to do otherwise. For if John's decision is undetermined, then the intervener won't be able to know what John's decision will be until he makes it. Then, if he waits until John decides, John's decision may be free but there *would* be alternative possibilities because the decision would be undetermined. In contrast, if John's choice is going to be undetermined and the intervener steps in to determine the choice to ensure he votes Republican, then there are no alternative possibilities for John. But his choice is not freely made by him nor is he responsible for his choice since the intervener has stepped in and made the choice for him.

PROF. RYAN: That's right. My point here is not original. A number of contemporary figures have made this sort of objection to Frankfurt scenarios like the one you've described. It has been called the "Indeterministic World Objection."

PROF. DANIELS: Hmm . . . I'm disappointed. I've been putting my faith in this kind of Frankfurt scenario.

PROF. RYAN: Don't be so glum. There may be ways around the Indeterministic World Objection. There are published responses, and the debate is ongoing.

PROF. DANIELS: Maybe I should look into this at some point.

PROF. RYAN: Maybe. But if you want to defend compatibilism, there are other worries you'll have to address, too.

PROF. DANIELS: Oh, what else? As if I haven't had a hard enough time dealing with the Consequence Argument.

PROF. RYAN: I think compatibilists have a hard time giving an adequate account of the criteria for free-willed action.

PROF. DANIELS: Really? What's on your mind here?

PROF. RYAN: Well, I missed the earlier part of your conversation. How did you define free-willed action?

JOHN (*butting into the conversation*): Professor Daniels said a person is free if and only if he has the power to do what he wants and there are no constraints preventing him from doing what he wants. So for instance, I'm freely here with you in the department lounge because I want to be here as opposed to being locked in here or being here due to a coercive threat, etc.

PROF. RYAN: I see. He stated the classical compatibilist position.

PROF. DANIELS: Yes, but I know this needs revision.

JOHN: Why?

PROF. RYAN: Shall I?

PROF. DANIELS: By all means.

PROF. RYAN: One significant problem with the classical compatibilist criterion is that it faces a problem with actions motivated by compulsive wants or desires. For instance, suppose I suffer from kleptomania. That is, suppose I have an overwhelming compulsive desire to steal things.

KATE: Oh, I see where you're going with this.

JOHN: I don't; clue me in.

KATE: John, do kleptomaniacs steal of their own free will?

JOHN: No, they can't help but steal due to their overwhelming compulsive desire to steal.

KATE: Exactly, but notice that when a kleptomaniac steals he does what he wants and he's not forced by any external sources or through coercive threat.

JOHN: Oh, I get it. So the classical compatibilist account would mistakenly label the kleptomaniac's stealing as free action.

KATE: Right.

PROF. RYAN: Nicely done, Kate.

KATE: Professor Daniels, you said you know the classical compatibilist view needs revision. Can it be modified to get around this problem?

PROF. DANIELS: Yes, I think so. In the recent literature there are a variety of revised compatibilist criteria of free action that are designed to avoid problems like this. Personally, I favor Frankfurt's view on this.

JOHN: Yes, what does he say?

PROF. DANIELS: Frankfurt distinguishes between two kinds of desires—first order desires and second order desires. He says first order desires are desires to act in certain ways, such as the desire to run, to sleep, to eat, etc., or to acquire certain things like food, money, and fame. Second order desires are desires to be moved or not moved by certain first order desires. For instance, I might be a heroin addict and consequently have a first order desire to take some heroin. But I might not want to be an addict, and so I might have a second order desire to not be moved to take heroin by this first order desire.

JOHN: Yes, I get this. Sometimes I find that I have desires to do things that I would prefer not to act on.

PROF. DANIELS: Yes, we have all experienced this from time to time.

JOHN: So how does all of this relate to the issue of free will?

PROF. DANIELS: According to Frankfurt, a person acts freely if and only if the first order desire that moves him to act is a desire that he can get to conform to his second order desires. Consider the kleptomaniac. The typical kleptomaniac realizes he has a problem and he would rather not be moved to steal by his compulsive desires to do so. On Frankfurt's view, such a kleptomaniac will not be said to act freely. He is moved to act by a first order desire to steal, but this is not a desire he can get to conform to his second order desire to not be moved by this desire.

JOHN: I see. The typical kleptomaniac does not want to be moved by these desires to steal but he cannot overcome these urges. Thus, when he acts on the first order desire to steal such action is not really expressive of his will. So in acting on these compulsive desires he does not exhibit free will.

PROF. DANIELS: Right, and notice that this is a *compatibilist* conception of free action. To act freely our actions need not be causally undetermined. Indeed, on this view it may be that all events, including all human actions, are determined. That's irrelevant to the freedom of human action. Rather, on this view an action must be caused in the right sort of way to be free. In particular, it must be caused by a first order desire that the agent can get to conform to his second order desires.

JOHN: Dr. Ryan, you said compatibilist theories have a hard time dealing with actions motivated by compulsive desires, such as the actions of kleptomaniacs. But here's a compatibilist account that solves this problem.

PROF. RYAN: Well, I said the *classical* compatibilists have a hard time dealing with these cases. Professor Daniels has presented us with a subtler kind of compatibilism that avoids this problem. Indeed, the view he has put forward has much to be said for it. For one thing, it draws to our attention the distinctive human ability to evaluate our first order desires with regard to our second order desires. No other animal seems to have this ability. Frankfurt's view ties this distinctive human ability to our capacity for free will and moral responsibility. But despite the subtlety and strength of this view, there are still good reasons to reject it.

PROF. DANIELS: Well, come on, out with it.

JOHN AND KATE: Yes, do tell.

PROF. RYAN: It seems to me that with regards to views like Frankfurt's we need to be concerned with the causal origins of the second order desires that are used to evaluate our first order desires.

PROF. DANIELS: What do you have in mind?

PROF. RYAN: Perhaps an example would help. Suppose that John here was raised in a cult-like community; he and his parents and everyone in his village are members. Suppose that in this community boys are taught to treat women as inferior and they are made to desire to treat them as inferior. Also, suppose that the brainwashing of the children in this village is so thorough that not only do the boys desire to treat women as inferior—a first order desire—but they also desire to be moved by such desires. That is, the boys in this community have been led to desire to treat women as inferior and they want to be moved by this desire, but they have been brainwashed by their elders in such a way that this is the inevitable consequence of the way they are raised.

It seems to me that the boys in this community will treat women as inferior because they desire to do so, and in acting in this way from such a desire their actions conform to their second order desires, since they want to be moved by the desire to treat women as inferior. In Frankfurt's view, we'd have to regard such actions of the boys in this community as free willed. But it's obvious that such action is not free willed, since it is the inevitable consequence of brainwashing.

PROF. DANIELS: But this seems ridiculous. This level of brainwashing cannot be achieved. Surely, all human beings will have some level of responsibility for what first and second order desires they have. These desires cannot be the inevitable result of social engineering.

PROF. RYAN: It's an interesting question about brainwashing—its nature and how it happens. But regardless, let me make two points. First, whether this level of brainwashing can actually happen is beside the point. The point is to imagine that this logically possible scenario did occur. If so, those who hold Frankfurt's view would be led to say the boys in this community act freely. Yet this seems obviously wrong. Second, I do think this kind of brainwashing can and does occur. One aspect of the Nazi regime's rise to power involved brainwashing. Children were taught to desire to treat Jews as inferior, and they were taught to admire the high-ranking members of the Nazi Party. The joint effect of this may have been to create children who not only desired to treat Jews as inferior but who also desired to be moved by this desire so that they might be like the high-ranking members of the Nazi party whom they admired.

PROF. DANIELS: Well said. I see your point. I've got to get going. Let me just say that despite the points that have been made here, I still can't help thinking that compatibilism is on the right track.

PROF. RYAN: You're not alone. It's a view that's had a lot of traction in the philosophical community, especially in recent years. If I've dissuaded you from Frankfurt's compatibilism, you could always consider the compatibilist views of others, such as Daniel Dennett, Owen Flanagan, Gary Watson, or Susan Wolf.

I, for one, don't spend a lot of time studying their work, because I don't think compatibilists can answer the Consequence Argument—an argument that turned me into a committed incompatibilist.

PROF. DANIELS: We'll have to discuss your views some other time. See you.

Prof. Daniels departs.

PROF. RYAN: John, Kate, do you want to carry the conversation further?

JOHN: No, it's about time to head to Bennett Hall for dinner. It's steak night.

PROF. RYAN: Oh, yeah, steak night! I almost forgot. May I join you?

JOHN: Please do, but can we switch to a lighter subject to discuss over dinner?

KATE: Yeah, we're a little worn out.

PROF. RYAN: Okay, sure. Say, did I tell you the one about the . . . .

John, Kate, and Prof. Ryan exit as Prof. Ryan relates one of the many jokes he loves to tell.

Scene 2

Wednesday, 10 p.m. John and Kate have been studying together in the library. John is sitting at a table reading. Kate is not there, but her books are on the table next to John's. Kate enters and puts her cell phone into her backpack, and takes a seat across from John.

JOHN: Man, you were gone for almost an hour. Who called?

KATE: You're not gonna believe this.

JOHN: Try me.

KATE: That was my father.

JOHN: You're kidding. Really?

KATE: Yep.

JOHN: What did he want?

KATE: He says he's coming to visit.

JOHN: Do you want him to?

KATE: I don't know. Not really.

JOHN: Did you tell him you don't want to see him?

KATE: That's just it. I tried to, but then he started getting upset. And he talked about how sorry he was for the way he treated me and the rest of my family. I felt so bad for him. I guess I just caved in.

JOHN: When's he coming?

KATE: Weekend after next.

JOHN: What are you gonna do?

KATE: I don't know. Maybe I'll just play nice. Show him around the campus. Take him to the choir concert. Maybe ignore the past. What would you do?

JOHN: Slug him in the nose.

KATE: Ha! Yeah, right.

JOHN: Well, your strategy of ignoring the past when he visits might work temporarily. But that won't work forever. You told me how bad he made you feel years ago. Eventually, those issues will need to be addressed.

KATE: I know. Eventually, if I'm ever going to have a relationship with him again I have to figure out whether I can forgive him. Right now, I don't know if I want that.

JOHN: It stinks having to deal with this in the middle of the semester.

KATE: Don't I know it.

John yawns and stretches in his seat and closes his book.

JOHN: Well, I've had enough intellectual stimulation for the day. The Beta house awaits. Care to join? Might help to get your mind off your dad.

KATE: No, I've still got thirty pages of Tillich to read for tomorrow.

JOHN: Better you than me. (*John pauses.*) Kate, you might want to talk with someone about your father's upcoming visit.

KATE: Yeah, maybe. See you.

JOHN (*smiling*): It's getting late. Gotta go gather some more of those rose buds while I may.

Kate smiles and John exits.

Study Questions

1. Define compatibilism and provide the classical compatibilist definition of free will.

2. According to Prof. Daniels, what kind of considerations suggest the classical compatibilist definition of free will is correct?

3. Explain the Consequence Argument.

4. Explain the conditional analysis of "could have done otherwise." How might this help the compatibilist answer the Consequence Argument?

5. Explain Prof. Daniels' critique of the conditional analysis of "could have done otherwise."

6. Explain the alternative way of responding to the Consequence Argument that Prof. Daniels endorses. Also, explain the two different strategies he uses in defending this response. What criticisms of these two different strategies are offered up by Profs. Goldfarb and Ryan?

7. According to Prof. Ryan, how does a phenomenon such as kleptomania present a problem for classical compatibilism?

8. Explain Frankfurt's account of the nature of free-willed action and how it avoids the problem of kleptomania, which classical compatibilism faces.

9. Explain Prof. Ryan's critique of the Frankfurtian view of free-willed action.

Discussion Questions

1. Is the Consequence Argument sound? Explain.

2. Does Prof. Daniels give an adequate refutation of the conditional analysis of "could have done otherwise"? Explain.

3. Do Frankfurt-type examples show that free will does not require alternative possibilities? Why or why not?

4. In Act 1, it is argued that those who believe free-willed acts are causally undetermined face the problem of luck. In Act 2, compatibilism— the view that free-willed acts may be causally determined—also faces some stiff criticism. Keeping this in mind, should we just embrace hard incompatibilism? Why or why not? Explain.

Suggestions for Further Reading

For articulations and defenses of classical compatibilism from the 17th, 18th, and 19th centuries, respectively, see Thomas Hobbes' *Leviathan* (1958 [1651]), Pt. II, Ch. 21; David Hume's *An Enquiry Concerning Human Understanding* (1974 [1748]), Sect. VIII; and John Stuart Mill's *A System of Logic* (1874), especially VI, ii, 3. For twentieth-century defenses of classical compatibilism, see A.J. Ayer (1954), J.J.C. Smart (1963), G.E. Moore (1912), and Kai Nielsen (1971).

The classic statement of the Consequence Argument is found in recent writings by Peter Van Inwagen (1983, 2002). This argument has also been defended by Carl Ginet (1990). As noted in Act 2, there are at least two ways of responding to the Consequence Argument: one way is to present and defend the conditional analysis of "could have done otherwise"; the other is to argue that free will does not require the capacity to do otherwise. For conditional analyses of "could have done otherwise," see Ayer (1954) and Nielsen (1971). The criticism of the conditional analysis comes from Michael McKenna (2004). For another critique of the conditional analysis, see Roderick Chisholm (1964). It is noted that there have been recent attempts to revive the conditional analysis of "could have done otherwise"; see Michael Fara (2008) and Kadri Vihvelin (2004). A nice discussion of these recent conditional analyses can be found in Bernard Berofsky (2011).

For defenses of the view that free will does not require the capacity to do otherwise, see Daniel Dennett (1984a,b) and Harry Frankfurt (1969). The criticism of Dennett's view found in Act 2 is derived from Robert Kane (2005, Ch. 8); also see Kane, "Some Neglected Pathways in the Free Will Labyrinth" (2002a), pp. 406–37. The Indeterministic World Objection to Frankfurt's argument that free will does not require alternative possibilities has been expressed by Robert Kane (1985), David Widerker (1995), Carl Ginet (1996), and Keith Wyma (1997). For replies to the Indeterministic World Objection, see David Hunt (2000, 2005), Mele and Robb (1998), Derk Pereboom (2001), and Eleonore Stump (1995, 1996). For some collections of readings dealing with Frankfurt-type examples, see David Widerker and Michael McKenna (2003) and John Martin-Fischer and Mark Ravizza (1993). In Act 2 consideration is given to Harry Frankfurt's compatibilist account of the nature of free-willed action. The classic statement of his view can be found in his "Freedom of the Will and the Concept of a Person" (1971). The criticism of this view is derived from points made in Richard Double (1991). For a related critique, see Gary Watson (1975). Robert Kane (2005, Ch. 9) has a good summary of the relevant concerns regarding this issue. For alternative compatibilist accounts of the nature of free-willed action, see Daniel Dennett (1984a,b, 2003), Owen Flanagan (2002, Ch. 4), Gary Watson (1975), and Susan Wolf (1987, 1990).

A theory not considered in Act 2 but which is worthy of serious consideration is semi-compatibilism. As suggested by the name, the theory is akin to compatibilism in some respects, but it is also different from it in significant ways. John Martin Fischer is the most prominent advocate of this view. He believes moral responsibility is compatible with determinism but that freedom is not compatible with it. He appeals to Frankfurt-type examples in arguing that responsibility and freedom are compatible, but he also argues that freedom requires alternative possibilities in a way that is inconsistent with determinism. See John Martin Fischer (1994, 1999, 2006) and John Martin Fischer and Mark Ravizza (1998).

Prof. Ryan's assertion that compatibilism is a "wretched subterfuge" is taken from Immanuel Kant's famous remark on this view; see Kant's *Critique of Practical Reason* (1956 [1788]). Finally, it is noted that Frankfurt-type examples develop a point that was originally considered by John Locke in the seventeenth century. The relevant source is Locke's *An Essay Concerning Human Understanding* (1690), Bk. II, Ch. 2.

Act 3: Libertarianism

Scene 1

Friday, 4 p.m. John is seated at a table in a small classroom. There are various documents strewn out over the table. John is joined by Armando and Jenny, the other two members of the student judicial board.

JOHN: Well, it looks like we're in agreement then.

JENNY: I don't see how we could decide the case in any other way.

ARMANDO: Yeah, I mean the central thesis of her paper is taken right out of the journal article Professor Arnold showed us.

JENNY: And she just cut and pasted three whole pages of that journal article right into her own paper and never cited that source anywhere in her paper.

It's a clear and obvious case of plagiarism.

ARMANDO: Yep.

JOHN: I agree. We have no choice but to find her guilty of the charge.

JENNY: I wonder why she chose to have her case heard by us. She could have just had the dean deal with it.

JOHN: Jenny, you know how it is. A lot of students think we'll be softer on them than the dean.

JENNY: I suppose.

ARMANDO: It's funny that students think we'll be soft on them. There's no evidence that supports that view.

JOHN: I know.

Well, before we bring her in to give her the verdict, let's talk about a meeting time for the punitive deliberations. Can you guys meet on Monday at 4 p.m.?

Armando and Jenny check their schedules.

ARMANDO: I'm good with that.

JENNY: Me too.

JOHN: Okay, good. Armando, will you go tell Janet we're ready?

Armando goes to the door, opens it, and waves Janet Richardson into the room. Janet enters and sits in the chair in front of the table where John sits, flanked by Armando and Jenny.

JOHN: Janet, we've heard testimony today from you and Professor Arnold. We have also completed a thorough investigation of the textual evidence Professor Arnold gave us, supporting his charge of plagiarism.

After deliberation, we've decided to find you guilty of the charge.

Janet very momentarily begins to sob out loud, but composes herself quickly while a few tears roll down her cheek. Armando grabs a tissue box and carries it to her, and she wipes her eyes.

JOHN: As is the custom with a judicial board case, the board will take a couple of days to consider the case before deciding on punitive measures. We'll be able to let you know the punishment at some point later next week.

JANET: My God. Is expulsion a possibility?

JOHN: Yes, it is.

Another sob escapes from Janet, but again she composes herself quickly.

JOHN: Do you have any other questions?

JANET: No.

JOHN: It is also the custom of the judicial board to give the convicted a final opportunity to explain themselves before adjourning. Is there anything you want to say?

JANET: Yes, there is.

Janet takes a moment to compose herself.

JANET: My . . . my life is hell, and this episode is surely only making it worse. In deliberating about my punishment, I only ask that each of you try to better understand me through what I'm about to tell you.

First of all, you're right. I'm guilty, guilty as hell. I knew what I did was wrong. It's not the first time that I've done this sort of thing. It's not even the first time I've done this sort of thing at this college.

You see, in my high school kids cheated all the time. It was commonplace. Kids hardly ever got caught, and when they were caught the punishment was so light that it was a joke. That's where I started cheating, in my high school. You're probably surprised to hear this. I think a lot of people who know me would be surprised to hear this. Everyone thinks I have it all together—that I'm so smart and stable and well adjusted.

Janet pauses and wipes away a few tears.

JANET: But I'm not. I'm not smart and well adjusted. I'm miserable.

If you . . . if you only knew the kind of pressure and expectations my parents place on me and have placed on me for so long, then you'd understand why I cheat and why I did what I did. When I don't cheat and I get B's; that's never good enough for them. It's always, "Dammit, Janet, you're a Richardson. Richardsons settle for nothing but excellence!" Or, "You'll never get into medical school with scores like those."

Janet pauses again.

JANET: It's awful. I try to tell them science is not my thing, but they just don't listen. And now that I've been taking so many science classes and struggling with them, my GPA is in jeopardy. If I don't keep my GPA up, I'm in danger of losing my scholarship, and my parents can't afford the tuition here without that scholarship. I've been under a lot of pressure for a long time and things are even worse this semester.

She stops to wipe away a few more tears.

JANET: Christ. Just look at me now. Please just try to understand these things before deciding on a punishment.

Janet stands up and leaves the room.

Scene 2

Saturday, 4:30 p.m. It's a lovely spring afternoon. The annual philosophy department picnic is being held on campus on the quad near St. Mark's Hall. John and Kate find Prof. Ryan seated at the base of a large tree with some other students. John and Kate decide to join them.

PROF. RYAN: John, Kate. Glad you could make it. Good to see you.

KATE: Yes, it's a beautiful day.

JOHN: Yeah, who could miss such good company on such a great spring day?

PROF. RYAN: Well, I'm glad some folks enjoy the company of philosophers. Not everyone does, you know.

JOHN: Yes, I took your course on Plato. It's hard to forget what happened to Socrates.

PROF. RYAN: Hmm . . . yes. I sometimes wonder if the administrators of this college wouldn't put me to death if they could.

KATE: Oh, Dr. Ryan, they've got too much respect for free and open discussion to look at things that way.

PROF. RYAN: I don't know. They grow awfully impatient with me at times.

JOHN: Well, if they come after you, we'll stand up for you.

PROF. RYAN: I'm sure you would. It's your nature to be protective of the ones you love.

KATE: Yes, it's his nature but he's not *necessitated* to act protectively, right, Dr. Ryan?

PROF. RYAN: Oh, this again? Are you still wondering about the nature of human action and whether all human decisions and actions are necessitated and whether there is any human freedom?

KATE: Well, as a matter of fact, yes. We are still wondering about this.

JOHN: Yeah, last night Kate and I were thinking back on the conversations we've had on this topic in the past few days, and we're seriously starting to question whether there is any human freedom or responsibility for action.

PROF. RYAN: Oh, why do you worry about this?

JOHN: We first started discussing the issues a few nights ago with Dr. Goldfarb. He argued that there is no human freedom, because human actions are either causally determined or they are not causally determined. He said that either way they are not free.

KATE: Yes, he said if our acts are causally determined then we cannot do otherwise and so we are not free, and if our acts are not causally determined then they are mere random occurrences, matters of luck, and we do not control them—meaning they are not free willed.

PROF. RYAN: Yes, this is the dilemma of determinism.

JOHN: Yeah, that's what Dr. Goldfarb called it, too. We couldn't find a way out of the problem.

PROF. RYAN: John, Kate, this is only a problem for you if you believe in free will. You could just adopt a view like Professor Goldfarb and embrace the argument.

JOHN: Well, we considered that but we're both uncomfortable with that option. We both feel that human beings really do possess a special capacity for free will that makes us morally responsible for many of our decisions and actions.

PROF. RYAN: Yes, I understand this feeling. I have it, too, and because of it I'm inclined to reject the dilemma of determinism.

KATE: But on what basis? It's not good enough to say, "Well, I just believe in human freedom and responsibility, so I reject the dilemma of determinism." It seems to me that an intellectually responsible reaction requires a well-reasoned argument.

JOHN: And as we listened to Professor Daniels explain and defend compatibilism the other day, we thought that this was the well-reasoned reply to be given to the dilemma of determinism. But then you and Professor Goldfarb pointed out what seemed to be gaping holes in the compatibilist view of things.

PROF. RYAN (*smiling*): Yes, well, sorry to burst your bubble there.

KATE: Well, now we don't know what to think.

PROF. RYAN: I see. You began to put your faith in the compatibilist defense of human freedom only then to be numbed by the barbs of the questions posed by Professor Goldfarb and myself.

JOHN: Exactly. Can you help us out here?

PROF. RYAN: Yes, I think so, but it won't be easy.

Professor Goldfarb approaches the group.

JOHN AND KATE: Hi, Professor Goldfarb. Would you care to join us?

PROF. GOLDFARB: I'd love to. My papers are graded, and I'm feeling footloose and fancy-free.

Professor Goldfarb sits down.

PROF. RYAN: John and Kate want me to provide a well-reasoned response to the dilemma of determinism.

PROF. GOLDFARB: Oh, I take it they were unimpressed with Professor Daniels' defense of compatibilism.

PROF. RYAN: That's right.

PROF. GOLDFARB (*to John and Kate*): Well, if compatibilism doesn't suit you then I'd have you seriously consider joining me in the hard incompatibilist camp. Because your only other option is **libertarianism**, and that view seems even more problematic than compatibilism.

PROF. RYAN: I disagree with you on the latter point. I think libertarianism provides a defensible solution to the dilemma of determinism.

JOHN: Wait a minute. What's this libertarian view you two are talking about?

PROF. RYAN: Recall that determinism is the view that at any moment in time the universe has exactly one physically possible future. So, for instance, many determinists believe all events, including human decisions and actions, are necessitated as the joint effects of the workings of prior events and the laws of nature.

JOHN: Yes, and compatibilists think human freedom and responsibility are consistent with this.

PROF. RYAN: Precisely, but in contrast libertarians believe human freedom and responsibility exist but that their existence is incompatible with determinism. Thus, they believe determinism is false. On their view, in order for human freedom and responsibility to exist at least some of our decisions and actions must not be causally determined.

KATE: This is basically the way that John and I conceptualized the nature of human freedom the other night when we were talking with Professor Goldfarb in the pub.

JOHN: Yes, but he argued that if human freedom is understood in this way then it cannot exist, because, as we said earlier, decisions and actions that are not causally determined are just random happenings—matters of luck or chance—that do not reflect the will of the agent. Thus, such decisions or acts cannot rightly be called free willed.

PROF. RYAN: And did Professor Goldfarb tell you that there are different kinds of libertarianism each with their own proposed solution to this problem of luck?

JOHN: No.

PROF. RYAN (*jokingly*): Jim, shame on you. You know the libertarian view deserves a fair consideration here.

PROF. GOLDFARB (*blushing*): I'm caught red-handed. But in all seriousness, I didn't explore those matters with them, because I don't think any of the libertarian options work.

KATE: What are the libertarian options?

JOHN: Yeah, do tell, Dr. Ryan.

PROF. RYAN: There are three main strands of libertarian thought, each of which has been defended in the recent literature on the subject. First, there is **agent-causal libertarianism**. On this view, free-willed acts are caused by persons, that is, agents who in acting freely act as uncaused causes of their actions. For instance, I'm presently thinking of going and getting a hot dog from our grill master over there. If I were to get up and do this of my own free will, then on the agent-causation view I, William Ryan, the person, would have to act as an uncaused cause of this action. That is to say, I would have to be the originating source of the action as opposed to any events, such as neurological events occurring in my brain.

JOHN: Wait a minute. Surely neurological events are causally involved in your actions, such as the act of going and getting a hot dog. If you get up and get a hot dog, then some event in your brain must trigger the sending of an electrical impulse along your nerves, stimulating the proper movements in your muscles, allowing you to go and get a hot dog. You aren't denying this, are you?

PROF. RYAN: Two points. First, I'm not defending the agent-causation theory. I'm just describing the view. Second, and more importantly, agent-causation theorists don't deny this. They would say that, of course, there are neurological events that occur in our brains that play a significant role in our free-willed behavior. But, on their view, no such events, indeed no events at all, can be the originating source of an action if it is a free-willed action. The originating source of an action must be the person—the continuously existing, substantial self—who in causing a free-willed action acts as an undetermined, uncaused cause of the act.

In freely going and getting a hot dog, I, William Ryan, the person, must begin a causal process that leads to my getting up and walking over and getting a hot dog. Presumably, I do something that triggers a series of neurological events that leads to my going and getting a hot dog.

KATE: It sounds like the agent-causation theorist must be committed to dualism about the self. The person or agent is some kind of nonphysical being that exists independent of the body and triggers the physical events that lead to the performance of our free-willed acts.

PROF. RYAN: Kate, the agent-causation theory can be conceived along the lines of dualism, but it doesn't have to be. Some contemporary agent-causation theorists argue that certain complex physical systems may have emergent properties that are not explainable with reference to the behavior of their parts. The functioning human brain, or at least parts of it, might be such a complex physical system, and the agent-causal power could be an emergent property of the brain, or at least certain parts of it.

JOHN: Dr. Ryan, for any libertarian view to be plausible it must be able to address the problem of luck, which we mentioned earlier. How does the agent-causal view deal with this?

PROF. RYAN: The problem of luck notes that if free-willed acts are not causally determined, then they are random occurrences unexpressive of the will of the agent. Thus, if not causally determined, then they are not free willed. The agent-causation theorist says free-willed acts are not causally determined, but they are still caused. They are caused by the agents who perform them. Since they are caused, they are not random. According to the agent-causation theory, in free-willed action the person (or agent) acts as an uncaused cause of his action. As such, free-willed acts are not determined, but they are still caused, and so they are not random occurrences either.

JOHN: Dr. Ryan, I assume you endorse some kind of libertarian position. Do you endorse agent-causal libertarianism?

PROF. RYAN: You're right. I do endorse libertarianism, but I'm not sure which version of the view is superior.

JOHN: Well then, you must have some reasons to doubt the agent-causal view. What are they?

PROF. RYAN: First, it doesn't sit well with a modern scientific worldview. Second, it doesn't really solve the luck problem. And third, the very idea of agent-causation is incoherent.

KATE: I think I know what you're getting at regarding agent causation not fitting with a modern scientific worldview. Scientists don't talk in terms of things or persons causing other things or events. Rather, they only talk in terms of certain events causing other events.

PROF. RYAN: Yes, this is exactly what I have in mind.

JOHN: I don't get that. It seems to me that substances—things—do cause events to happen. If you place a hot steel rod in water, the water—a substance—cools it. Thus, substances *do* have causal effects.

KATE: Yes, John, we *say* things like the water cools the steel, but from a modern scientific perspective that's misleading. What's really going on is the rapid movement in the atoms in the steel, which we perceive as hot, transfers movement to the atoms in the water. That is to say, certain events—movements in the atoms of steel—cause certain other events—movements in the atoms of the water. What we perceive as a reduction in the heat of the steel is really just a reduction in the movement of the atomic particles brought on by their transference of kinetic energy to the atoms in the water.

On the modern scientific worldview, all of the talk of substances causing things to happen is explainable in terms of certain events causing other events.

JOHN: Do you agree with this, Dr. Ryan?

PROF. RYAN: Yes, I do. And I think Kate has made the point quite nicely.

JOHN: Alright, I suppose the agent-causal theory may not fit in with a modern scientific worldview, but what about your second point? You also said the theory doesn't really solve the luck problem.

PROF. RYAN: Yes. The luck problem seeks to show that if free-willed acts are causally undetermined right up to the moment of choice, as libertarians maintain, then such choices would be random occurrences—matters of chance—unexpressive of the will of the agent. The agent-cause theorist comes along and says, "Yes, well, free-willed acts are undetermined at the moment of choice, but when the choice is made it's caused by the person, the agent. As such, it's under the control of the agent and it is not a random occurrence."

Consider the example I raised earlier. I considered going and getting a hot dog or staying and talking with you. I was torn between the two options, but I chose to stay and talk. According to agent-causal libertarianism, if this were a free choice, my choice must not have been determined by any beliefs or desires I had at the time of the choice—rather the choice must have been caused by me, Bill Ryan, the person, who acted as an uncaused cause in deciding to stay and talk.

JOHN: Right, and the idea here is that since you cause the choice, the choice is not a random or chance event. It's done with your control. What's wrong with this?

PROF. RYAN: Well, consider that in some other logically possible world there could be someone like me in all respects having all the same beliefs and desires and faced with the same choice. Since agent-caused decisions are the results of agents acting as uncaused causers, this means my doppelganger in another possible world could have chosen differently, even though everything about him was the same right up to the moment of choice.

KATE: I get it. The agent-causation theorist says your decision was not random—not a matter of luck—because it was caused by you. But since according to this view you act as an uncaused cause, this means someone just like you in every way could have chosen differently. And if so, then there's really nothing about you that explains your choice. Thus, even on the agent-causal theory, the choice still seems to be a random occurrence, a matter of luck—not really an expression of free will.

PROF. RYAN: Precisely.

JOHN: I see. This really does look like a serious problem.

PROF. RYAN: And that's not all. Remember, there was a third reason I had for doubting the agent-causal theory.

JOHN: Haven't you already heaped enough abuse on this theory?

PROF. RYAN: Do you want me to stop here?

KATE: No, I want to hear this third argument.

PROF. RYAN: John?

JOHN: If you must.

PROF. RYAN: Recall that the third problem suggests that the very idea of agent causation is incoherent. According to the agent-causation view, persons—beings, substances—cause free-willed actions, not events. Free-willed actions are themselves events. As such, they occur at specific times and places. If free-willed acts were caused by specific events occurring antecedent to them, then we could understand why they occur when they do. But agent-cause theorists believe free-willed acts are caused by persons not events. The problem here is that persons have an enduring existence long before and long after the free-willed acts associated with them. If free-willed acts are caused by persons, who are not events with a specific existence in time, then it's going to be impossible on the agent-cause theory to understand why free-willed acts occur at the times they actually occur.

John, you scratched your head moments ago. Now, if I say you're feeling an uncomfortable itch and your desire to relieve this itch caused the scratching, then I can easily make sense of why you scratched when you did as the itch and the desire occurred just antecedent to the scratching. But if, as the agent-cause theorists say, *you* caused the scratching, then we have a problem. You existed ten minutes ago and you weren't scratching. You exist now and you aren't scratching. So why did your scratching occur when it did if you were the only cause of it?

KATE: I see. Man, the agent-causation view certainly has a lot of problems. Wouldn't you agree, Professor Goldfarb?

PROF. GOLDFARB: Of course. Remember I'm a hard incompatibilist. I don't believe in the existence of human freedom. So I think all of the libertarian options are flawed.

PROF. RYAN: Well, I'm hungry and I'm going to freely proceed to the food line. John, Kate, will you join me?

JOHN AND KATE: Yes.

PROF. GOLDFARB: What about me?

PROF. RYAN: I suppose you will eat whenever the appropriate causal forces act upon you.

PROF. GOLDFARB: Well, they seem to be working fully well upon all of us right now. So I'll be joining you.

They proceed to the food line, and then they return to their seats with food, which they happily consume.

JOHN: Dr. Ryan, you said there were three main strands of libertarian thought. So far we've only talked about the agent-causal variety. Can you tell us about the other ones and which one you favor?

PROF. RYAN: Gladly.

KATE: Wait, before going on, I want to know something.

PROF. RYAN: Yes, Kate?

KATE: Have there been many noteworthy defenders of the agent-causal theory and does anyone still embrace the view?

PROF. RYAN: Oh, sure. In the eighteenth century, the view was defended by George Berkeley and Thomas Reid. But there have been various recent and contemporary defenders of the view. Two of the most noteworthy contemporary defenders are Timothy O'Connor and Randolph Clarke, though the latter remains pretty skeptical about the prospects for the view. The view has also been given notable defenses in recent years by Roderick Chisholm, Richard Taylor, and William Rowe, among others. Many of these thinkers have proposed solutions to the problems I've raised here, but I remain doubtful about the effectiveness of their solutions.

KATE: Well, what about those other libertarian options you mentioned?

PROF. RYAN: The two other libertarian options are simple indeterminism and indeterministic event-causal libertarianism. I prefer the latter, but they both have some plausibility, and there are able contemporary advocates of both theories.

JOHN: Tell us about **simple indeterminism**, and then let's hear about your preferred view.

KATE: Yes, please.

PROF. RYAN: Alright. The simple indeterminist view is a libertarian view, which says that free-willed acts are undetermined because they are not caused at all. Recall that on the agent-causation view, free-willed acts are caused but they are caused by persons who act as uncaused causes, and thus, agent-caused acts are undetermined. In contrast, the simple indeterminist says free acts are not caused at all—not by earlier events, nor by states, nor by agents. This view is also known as "noncausal libertarianism."

KATE: Well, this certainly seems to be an odd view. Free-willed acts are not just random happenings. But this view, in saying they are uncaused, would seem to suggest as much.

PROF. RYAN: Yes, well, there's more to the view that addresses this point. Contemporary defenders of the view, such as Carl Ginet and Stewart Goetz, say that, while uncaused, free-willed acts are nonetheless done for certain reasons. Since free-willed acts are uncaused but done for reasons, they are undetermined yet not random.

Consider that in the lunch line moments ago I was given the option of a hamburger, a hot dog, or a fruit and cheese plate. I chose the hot dog. Now, if I did so freely, then on the simple indeterminist view the choice must have been uncaused. But to say it was uncaused is not to say it was a random occurrence, because my choice was made for certain reasons—in this case, the reason being I like hot dogs very much and more than the other options.

JOHN: But, Dr. Ryan, if that's the reason for your choice isn't it also the *cause* of the choice? Why shouldn't we just view reasons as the causes of intentional human behavior, such as your choice of a hot dog for lunch?

PROF. RYAN: That's a good question, John. Many people do look at the reasons we have for acting as the causes of our actions or, at least, as playing a causal role in our actions. But simple indeterminists, such as Ginet and Goetz, reject this idea, arguing that our reasons can play a significant role in explaining our behavior without that role being causal in any way. There's no doubt the view has been given some subtle defenses in the literature, but it has also been subjected to significant criticism.

JOHN: Such as?

PROF. RYAN: For one thing, I would note that, like the agent-causation view, simple indeterminism doesn't fit well with a modern scientific perspective. Modern science is premised upon the idea that everything that happens does so as a result of certain causal factors. Not all of these causes need to operate deterministically, as quantum physics suggests. Nonetheless, there are causes for all that happens in our universe, including human choices and actions.

Furthermore, simple indeterminism has trouble making sense of agent control of actions. Consider my choice of a hot dog for lunch. On the simple indeterminist view, if this is a free-willed choice, then the choice is uncaused. But it could be said that for the choice to be a product of my free will then I must control the choice, and to control the choice I, or at least some of my thought processes, must cause the choice. In this way it can be argued that the simple indeterminist view cannot make adequate sense of the agent control involved in free-willed choice and action.

JOHN: I see.

KATE: Me too. But I suppose that just as contemporary agent-causation theorists have responses to the objections against their view, the contemporary advocates of simple indeterminism have responses to these objections, too.

PROF. RYAN: Oh, sure. The debate between the different libertarian theorists and the compatibilists and the free-will skeptics, like Professor Goldfarb, is ongoing.

I don't think the agent-cause theorists or the simple indeterminists have given adequate answers to the problems I've presented, but maybe I'm wrong. If you find either of those views attractive, you might consider exploring the issues further by reading some of the recent literature on the subject. Personally, I prefer the third libertarian option—indeterministic event-causal libertarianism.

JOHN: Okay. So what is this view?

KATE: Yeah, tell us about it.

PROF. RYAN: This third view has been articulated quite well by a contemporary thinker named Robert Kane. On his view, in order for human freedom and responsibility to exist, some of our actions must be causally undetermined. And notice I say *some* of our actions must be causally undetermined. On Kane's view, many of the acts that we freely commit and for which we are responsible are causally determined. Such causally determined acts may have a derivative freedom and we may be responsible for them if they are determined by our character and if our character is the product of past causally undetermined free choices.

KATE: Yes, this makes sense to me. I expressed a similar view the other night when John and I were discussing the issues with Dr. Goldfarb. Remember?

PROF. GOLDFARB: Yes, I do.

KATE: It seems to me that a person's character is that set of beliefs and desires and dispositions of the will that leads him to choose and act as he does. A person's character may well necessitate many of the choices and actions that a person commits. But even if this is the case, it seems to me that one could be said to freely perform these necessitated acts and be responsible for them as long as he has committed causally undetermined free acts in the past that led to the shaping of that character.

JOHN: Right, the other day we considered the example of being offered a lot of money to torture an innocent person. If this money was offered to me, I couldn't bring myself to accept it and torture someone. My character won't allow me to. But we could say I freely refuse to accept the offer insofar as I have made free causally undetermined decisions in the past that have shaped the character I have today. Is this what Kane is saying?

PROF. RYAN: Yes, it is.

JOHN: I like this.

KATE: Me too. But it's still not clear what distinguishes this view from the agent-cause theory and simple indeterminism. Those theories could embrace these ideas while describing the character-forming undetermined decisions as agent caused or uncaused. I assume that on Kane's view the undetermined, character-forming decisions are not to be understood in this way.

PROF. RYAN: That's right, Kate. And that's certainly an astute observation.

JOHN: What's Kane's view on these undetermined, freely performed, character-shaping decisions?

PROF. RYAN: Kane calls them self-forming actions—SFAs—and he says they are causally undetermined decisions that are freely made by, and hence caused by, agents who make them. But unlike agent-causal and simple indeterminist views, Kane does not say that such decisions are not also caused by events involving the agents. Rather, on Kane's view free actions *are* caused by events involving the agent, but they are not causally determined. I think an example would help here. Let's see . . . I know. How's this?

Suppose on a Friday John promises his grandmother that he will mow her lawn on Sunday. On Saturday night his friends ask him to go fishing all day on Sunday. This leaves John feeling conflicted, since he very much wants to go fishing with his friends but he also feels obligated to mow his grandmother's lawn. Further, suppose his friends need to know right away whether he will join them on the trip. So John must decide whether to keep his promise to his grandmother or break the promise and go fishing.

JOHN: This scenario sounds all too familiar.

PROF. RYAN: I know. That's why I chose it.

KATE: Yes, but what's the point you want to make about Kane's view?

PROF. RYAN: Well, according to Kane, in cases like these where we feel conflicted about what to do because we have strongly motivating reasons to do two different actions and we cannot do both, we actually end up trying, or willing, to do both acts. So in this case, John actually tries, or wills, to keep his promise, and he tries, or wills, to break his promise.

Because in cases like these where we will to do both actions, each for different reasons, it is causally undetermined which action we end up performing. But whichever action we end up doing, the action will be caused by our willing it for certain reasons. Thus, in these situations our ultimate choice is caused by our willing, but the choice is undetermined, since it is not determined which of the competing wills is going to win out in the conflict to determine the choice. At the same time, whatever one ends up doing in a situation like this, it will still be under one's control since one wills his action for certain reasons of his own.

KATE: Oh, I see how the problem of luck is avoided here. According to this view, a causally undetermined decision is not a random decision, uncontrolled by the agent, because whatever the agent ends up deciding or doing, it will be a consequence of his willing it. So while it is causally undetermined whether John breaks his promise or not, whatever he does it will be expressive of his will either way. Even though the choice is undetermined, he controls what is done because we control whatever we will to do.

PROF. RYAN: That's right, Kate.

JOHN: Dr. Ryan, how exactly is this view of free-willed action different from the agent-causal and simple indeterminist views?

PROF. RYAN: The view I've just described is an indeterministic event-causal view. Each of the libertarian views we've looked at considers free-willed acts, or at least underivatively free acts, as undetermined. According to the simple indeterminist view, they are not caused at all. But on Kane's view, free-willed acts *are* caused but not deterministically caused. Furthermore, agent-causation theories also view free-willed acts as caused, but on these views they are caused not by events but by agents—persons. Agent-causation theorists do not believe the free-willed acts caused by persons can be understood in terms of event causes. In contrast, according to the Kanean view, free-willed acts are understood as caused by persons, *but* this causation by persons can be rightly understood in terms of event causation. On Kane's view, agents cause their free-willed acts, but they do so through their willing them and these willings are the event causes that underlie and explain agent causation.

JOHN: I see. And I suppose the idea here is that throughout our lives we perform many of these SFAs—self-forming acts—which are causally undetermined free-willed acts, and these play a role in shaping our character. So in our adult lives when our decisions are determined by our character, such that we cannot do otherwise, we are still responsible for these determined acts because we have freely shaped the character from which they proceed through our past SFAs. Is this right?

PROF. RYAN: Yes.

JOHN: I must say I find this view quite attractive.

KATE: Me too. Dr. Goldfarb, what do you think about this?

PROF. GOLDFARB: I'm skeptical.

PROF. RYAN: Oh? What troubles you about this view?

PROF. GOLDFARB: Well, for one thing, I would note that you criticized both the agent-causal and simple indeterminist views for being incompatible with a modern scientific worldview. I don't see how Kane's view fares any better on this front.

PROF. RYAN: Well, modern science is premised on the assumption that events, including human actions, are caused. The Kanean view is consistent with this assumption, but the simple indeterminist view is not consistent with it. Furthermore, the agent-causation view accepts an odd kind of causation between persons and events that doesn't fit within a modern scientific worldview. In contrast, on Kane's view all causation is between events, including the causation of free-willed actions.

PROF. GOLDFARB: Yes, in those respects Kane's view does fit better with a modern scientific worldview. But this view posits that in SFAs, mental events such as our willings or efforts indeterministically cause our actions. I think this is unscientific. Admittedly, quantum physics allows for some causal indeterminacy in the universe, but this occurs at the subatomic level. For the most part these subatomic indeterminacies are cancelled out when we examine the behavior and causes of larger objects and phenomena.

PROF. RYAN: Have you ever heard of chaos theory?

PROF. GOLDFARB: Yes, but I don't know much about it.

PROF. RYAN: Well, I'm hardly an expert on it either. But I would note that Kane says there is some scientific evidence suggesting that chaos and quantum-level indeterminacy might make room for higher-level causal indeterminacy. In chaotic physical systems, very small changes in initial conditions lead to large and unpredictable changes in the system's subsequent behavior. There is limited scientific data suggesting that under certain conditions chaotic states in the neurons of our brains may allow for the magnification of quantum level indeterminacies in brain functioning. Such chaotic states my well exist in neuronal functioning when we are faced with the kinds of vexing decisions we encounter in self-forming acts—the SFAs we were talking about moments ago. If so, then in these situations the choices we ultimately make may well be causally undetermined.

PROF. GOLDFARB: I don't know, Bill. All of this sounds pretty speculative.

PROF. RYAN: Yes, it is pretty speculative. But you were suggesting that the Kanean view doesn't fit with a modern scientific worldview any better than other libertarian views. I'm just trying to show that, one, it does not disagree with any fundamental assumptions of modern science in the way the other libertarian views do and, two, there are some limited scientific findings that may support the Kanean view. Admittedly, the findings are minimal. But neuroscience and chaos theory are young disciplines. In time, there may be more scientific findings that support the view. We'll have to wait and see.

PROF. GOLDFARB: Hmm . . . well, you've certainly made some good points here. I suppose the view does fit better with a modern scientific worldview than the other views. But it's still speculative.

PROF. RYAN: Agreed.

PROF. GOLDFARB: But there *is* something else that bothers me about this view . . .

PROF. RYAN: Yes, go on.

PROF. GOLDFARB: Well, I can see you want to say that even though SFAs are undetermined they are not random nor matters of luck or chance, because the agent wills to do both of two possible actions, only one of which can actually be done. Consequently, while the agent's ultimate action is undetermined he controls what he does, since he wills it either way. What we do as a matter of our own control is not random nor merely a matter of luck. Thus, we can say that, although they are undetermined, SFAs are nonetheless free-willed acts for which we are responsible.

I can see that if this reasoning is sound, then it forms a response to one side of the dilemma of determinism, which is the ultimate basis for my own skepticism about the existence of free will.

PROF. RYAN: That's right. And this should bother you. But I take it you don't think the reasoning is sound.

PROF. GOLDFARB: No, I don't.

PROF. RYAN: Why not?

PROF. GOLDFARB: The dual willing idea seems implausible. I mean, think about it. When we are faced with these vexing, difficult decisions in life we don't experience ourselves as willing both of two acts. Going back to our earlier example, if John is faced with the difficult decision of keeping his promise to his grandmother or going fishing with his friends instead, he doesn't will to do both acts.

JOHN (*butting in*): Hey, you're right. Rather, in these situations it seems to me that I want to do both, or maybe I want to do one and feel obligated to do another, but I don't experience myself as trying or willing to do both. Instead, it seems that I just will to do one of these two things, each of which I am strongly motivated to do.

PROF. RYAN: I see. Well, admittedly we don't usually experience ourselves as willing both acts in these dilemmatic situations, but that doesn't mean we are not willing both acts. There's a lot that goes on in our mental lives that we are unaware of—dual willings might well just be another instance of this. Consider that in visual perception the brain separately processes different features of the visual scene, such as object and background. This separate processing occurs, but we are unaware of it. Furthermore, the fact that we are unaware of it is not a good argument against its occurrence. Thus, to say that we are unaware of any dual willings that occur when we face a dilemmatic choice is not a good argument against the existence of such dual willing.

JOHN: I think he's got us there, Dr. Goldfarb.

PROF. GOLDFARB: Maybe. I'll have to think about it. Right now I want to raise one other concern I have about this view.

PROF. RYAN: Yes, Jim, what is it?

PROF. GOLDFARB: Even if I grant that dual willings occur in SFAs, I'm still concerned that on this view free-willed acts are random or arbitrary occurrences, suggesting a loss of agent control and a loss of responsibility. Again, going back to the example of John who must choose to keep his promise to his grandmother or go fishing, suppose he does, as you say, will both acts and he ultimately chooses to keep his promise. According to your view this choice is undetermined right up to the moment of choice. But if so, then someone in another logically possible world who is just like John in every way and who confronts the exact same choice could choose differently. This implies that there is really nothing about the psychological states of John leading up to the moment of his choice that can explain why the one choice is made as opposed to the other. We won't be able to explain why he chooses to keep his promise as opposed to going fishing. Thus, the Kanean view makes free-willed acts arbitrary in this way, suggesting a lack of agent control over the choice and a lack of responsibility for it.

PROF. RYAN: An interesting point, Jim. But I think it can be answered.

PROF. GOLDFARB: Have at it.

Professor Ryan picks up a dead tree limb off the ground.

PROF. RYAN: Suppose that some days my muscles are weaker than on other days, and it is indeterminate as to when they are weaker and when not. Okay?

PROF. GOLDFARB: Okay.

PROF. RYAN: And suppose now I try to snap this limb in two.

PROF. GOLDFARB: Yes.

PROF. RYAN: And let us suppose, then, that it is causally indeterminate as to whether I will have the strength to do so.

PROF. GOLDFARB: Okay.

PROF. RYAN: And suppose that I go ahead and break it. Then, would I be responsible for breaking it?

PROF. GOLDFARB: Yes, of course.

PROF. RYAN: I quite agree with you. But notice, the breaking of it was not causally determined, since it was undetermined whether I would have the strength to do so. So you see, my friend, we can be fully responsible for the doing of things that are not causally determined.

JOHN: Dr. Ryan, can you relate this to SFAs and Dr. Goldfarb's objection?

PROF. RYAN: I'm getting there, John. Geez, Rome wasn't built in a day. What's with these kids today, Jim?

PROF. GOLDFARB: Too many energy drinks and video games.

PROF. RYAN: Ha! Yes. Well, look, the point is that a Kanean may concede that there is some loss of agent control in the undetermined choices made in the contexts of SFAs. The fact that we cannot explain why one choice ultimately gets made over the other suggests some arbitrariness and some loss of control in free-willed action. *But* it suggests no loss of responsibility for the choice that gets made. Just as I can be fully responsible for my causally undetermined breaking of the tree limb, so too can John be fully responsible for his causally undetermined decision to keep his promise. In both cases, we are responsible for the same reason—because we willed the doing of our acts.

JOHN: So according to the indeterministic event-causal libertarian view there is some diminished agent control over free-willed decisions but no diminished responsibility?

PROF. RYAN: That's right. On this view, the diminished control we have is just part of the price we pay for possessing free will and responsibility. I might add the price seems worth it, as somehow life seems more interesting and worthwhile if we have such freedom and responsibility.

JOHN: I agree. Dr. Goldfarb, what about you?

PROF. GOLDFARB: I don't know what to think. I suspect foul play in the argument here, but I don't know what it is.

Silence falls over the group for a while, as they think about the issues.

KATE: Professor Ryan, this Kanean event-causal libertarianism has a lot of intuitive appeal and it seems to be immune to objections. Is it the most popular and plausible view on free will these days?

PROF. RYAN: Oh, heavens no, Kate. It's certainly not the most popular view among philosophers. Many philosophers feel it is too speculative and that the luck problem remains a stumbling block. Furthermore, it's hard to say whether it is even the most plausible view.

I like the view because, one, I'm inclined to think we have free will; two, I don't think compatibilists can answer the Consequence Argument; and, three, of all the libertarian views, I think the event-causal variety fits the best with a modern scientific worldview. But there are other plausible event-causal libertarian theories, such as those of Mark Balaguer and Laura Ekstrom. And other kinds of libertarians have been working hard to make their views more consistent with a scientific worldview. For instance, Timothy O'Connor has been doing this for the agent-causal brand of libertarianism.

JOHN: Well, I see that you think there are other plausible libertarian views. But would you say libertarian views are more plausible than the other views on free will, such as compatibilism and free-will skepticism?

PROF. RYAN: Like I said, I prefer the libertarian approach and I've explained why. But it's too hard to know at this point which libertarian view is best or even whether libertarianism is superior to compatibilism or free-will skepticism. The debate is ongoing.

JOHN: But you seem to have given good answers to all the objections presented here today.

PROF. RYAN: Sure, things may seem this way and maybe I have given good answers. But believe me, there are lots of other objections to the Kanean view, which we haven't even considered here. Some of them run very deep, and it's not clear whether the Kanean view can answer all of them.

Silence falls over the group again.

PROF. RYAN: Well, I've got to get going. It's been a pleasure.

Prof. Ryan walks off in the direction of his car.

PROF. GOLDFARB: Well kids, it's been fun. Better yet I've been given a lot to think about. I'm glad I have a colleague like Bill around to challenge my settled opinions. It invites re-examination of my own beliefs and keeps me humble.

KATE: We understand. It's why we keep coming back for more philosophy classes.

PROF. GOLDFARB: Enjoy the day!

JOHN AND KATE: Bye.

Prof. Goldfarb heads in the direction of his office in St. Mark's Hall. John and Kate sit quietly for a moment, absorbed in their thoughts and appreciating the beauty of the day. After a while they look at each other and smile.

JOHN: Frisbee?

KATE: Sure.

Study Questions

1. Define libertarianism.

2. Define agent-causal libertarianism, and explain how it tries to answer the problem of luck.

3. Explain the three objections to the agent-causation theory presented by Prof. Ryan.

4. Define simple indeterminist libertarianism, and explain how it tries to answer the problem of luck.

5. Explain the two objections to the simple indeterminist theory presented by Prof. Ryan.

6. Explain the event-causal libertarian view, which Prof. Ryan defends. How does it try to answer the problem of luck?

7. Explain Prof. Goldfarb's three objections to Prof. Ryan's preferred libertarian theory. Explain Prof. Ryan's replies to each of these.

Discussion Questions

1. Prof. Ryan maintains that the event-causal libertarian view is an improvement on the other two libertarian views he considers. Is he right about this? Explain your answer.

2. Does Prof. Ryan's preferred event-causal libertarian view—the Kanean view—really solve the problem of luck? Why or why not?

3. Do you accept Prof. Ryan's response to the objection that we don't experience ourselves as willing both acts in the face of dilemmatic choice? Explain your answer.

4. Is Prof. Ryan right to maintain that we can be fully responsible for our choices even if there is some arbitrariness, that is, randomness, in the ultimate choices we make? What do you think of the example of the causally undetermined breaking of a stick, which he uses in supporting his position? Is the example appropriate? Explain your answers.

Suggestions for Further Reading

For a good short survey of libertarian theories of free will, see Randolph Clarke, "Incompatibilist (Nondeterministic) Theories of Free Will" (2008) in *The Stanford Encyclopedia of Philosophy*, which is available on the web. Clarke's essay contains a very thorough bibliography, covering the different libertarian options. Kane (2005) also provides a nice survey of the different libertarian options; see especially Ch. 4–6 and 11–12. Different libertarian theories are explained and critiqued in each of the following works: Randolph Clarke (2003), Laura Ekstrom (2000), and Timothy O'Connor (2000).

For some eighteenth-century defenses of the agent-causation theory, see George Berkeley ([1710], 1998) and Thomas Reid ([1788], 1969). For more recent and contemporary defenses of the view, see Roderick Chisholm (1964, 1976), Randolph Clarke (2003), Timothy O'Connor (2000), William Rowe (1991, 2000, 2006), and Richard Taylor (1966, 1992). The argument that agent-causal theories do not fit well with a modern scientific worldview is expressed in the writings of Daniel Dennett (2003), Owen Flanagan (2002), and Robert Kane (1996, 2007). The argument that agent-causal theories cannot solve the problem of luck is presented by Ishtiyaque Haji (2004), Alfred Mele (2005, 2006), and Peter Van Inwagen (1983, 2002). The coherence problem faced by agent-causal views, which is concerned with explaining the timing of free-willed acts, has been presented by C.D. Broad (1952) and Carl Ginet (1990, 1997).

Simple indeterminist (or noncausalist) libertarian views have been defended by Carl Ginet (1990, 1997), Stewart Goetz (1988, 1997), and Hugh McCann (1998). The argument that simple indeterminist views have trouble accounting for agent control of free-willed acts has been made by Timothy O'Connor (2000).

As noted in Act 3, the event-causal libertarian view that Prof. Ryan prefers is that of Robert Kane. Kane's view has been defended by him in many works; see, for instance, Robert Kane (1996, 2002a, 2007). The argument that the Kanean idea of dual willing does not fit with the facts of our experience of dilemmatic choice has been expressed by Laura Ekstrom (2003). The argument that Kane's theory faces problems of luck and arbitrariness has been presented by Randolph Clarke (1999, 2002, 2003), Meghan Griffith (2010), Ishtiyaque Haji (1999), Alfred Mele (1999a,b), and Timothy O'Connor (1996). For additional discussion of the Kanean view and the problem of luck, see John Lemos (2007, 2011a,b).

For defenses of other kinds of event-causal libertarian views, see Mark Balaguer (2010), Laura Ekstrom (2000, 2003), and David Hodgson (2012). Although there are significant differences between Kane's and Balaguer's views, Balaguer's view is like Kane's in the sense that he believes free-willed acts can be causally undetermined right up to the moment of choice. In contrast, Ekstrom puts forward an event-causal theory in which the causal indeterminacy of free-willed acts occurs not at the moment of choice but in the deliberative process leading up to the choice. This kind of view has also been developed and discussed by Alfred Mele (1995, 1996, 2006) and Daniel Dennett (1978), and more recently by Bob Doyle (2011).

Toward the end of Act 3, Prof. Ryan notes that there are several objections to the Kanean view that have not been considered in the discussion. For examples of these, see Randolph Clarke (2002), Alfred Mele (2006), John Lemos (2011b), and Neil Levy (2005). It is also noted that Timothy O'Connor has been working to make the agent-causal brand of libertarianism more scientifically respectable; see O'Connor (2000, 2009, 2011).

Act 4: Free Will and Science

Scene 1

Monday, 11 a.m. John and Kate are walking on campus after one of their classes together.

JOHN: Kate, did you ever find someone to talk to about your dad?

KATE: Yep. I'm going to see the chaplain this afternoon.

JOHN: Good move. I know you two get along well.

KATE: Yeah, it'll be good to catch up with her. I haven't seen her in a few weeks.

John grows quiet and Kate notices.

KATE: What?

JOHN: You know, I don't think the chaplain likes me very much.

KATE: Don't be silly. Why would you say that?

JOHN: I get the sense she thinks I'm not sufficiently committed to Christian values nor sufficiently sympathetic toward religious worldviews in general.

KATE: Well, you're not.

JOHN: I think we should love our neighbors as ourselves.

KATE: And do you live by this?

JOHN: Yes, especially when my neighbor is an attractive young female with a taste for philosophical discussions and a love for rock and roll.

KATE: Geez, and you wonder why the chaplain might be cold toward you.

JOHN: What? Now it's you, too?

KATE: Don't worry. I know your values are better than you let on.
    Hey, I'm going rock climbing with the Federation of Christian Athletes later this afternoon around 4 o'clock. You wanna join us?

JOHN: I'd love to, but I've got a J-board meeting.

KATE: That's too bad. Is it a new case?

JOHN: No, same one. Today we have to decide on punitive measures. I'm not looking forward to it. The issues are pretty serious.

KATE: Oh, so we're not talking public urination this time.

JOHN: Afraid not.

KATE: Well, good luck with it. I'm off to the library. See you.

JOHN: Yeah, see you.

John and Kate head their separate ways.

Scene 2

Monday, noon. John and his friend Brian, a chemistry major, are having lunch in Bennett Hall.

JOHN: Brian, where were you this weekend? Kate and I stopped by your room a few times, but you were nowhere to be seen.

BRIAN: I went home to see my sister perform in a school play and to help my mom move some old furniture out of the house.

You said you were going to the philosophy department picnic this weekend. How was that?

JOHN: It was fun. Dr. Ryan held court on the subject of free will. Man, I'm glad I decided to major in philosophy. I love the issues we get to explore.

BRIAN: Yeah, but do you guys ever really prove anything? What's the point of all these long philosophical debates if nothing ever gets resolved?

JOHN: Here you go again with the scientific skepticism about philosophy. Don't you realize that some questions are worth asking and contemplating even if they are not empirically resolvable?

BRIAN: Let's not go there again. So what did Dr. Ryan say about free will?

JOHN: He endorsed a libertarian theory of free will. According to this view, in order for humans to exhibit freedom and for them to be responsible for their actions at least some of the actions they perform must be causally un-determined free acts.

BRIAN: So, according to this view, in order for me to have free will some of my actions have to be undetermined by any beliefs or desires I have and/or any neurological states of my brain prior to decision and action?

JOHN: That's right.

BRIAN (*sarcastically*): What will these philosophers think of next?

JOHN: What's with your skepticism?

BRIAN: John, such a view just isn't intellectually respectable.

JOHN: You're not advocating determinism, are you?

BRIAN: You should know me better than that. We've covered this ground before. We agree that there's no good reason to think *all* events in the universe are causally determined.

JOHN: Right, given the findings of quantum physics, it follows that, for all we know, there may be some phenomena at the subatomic level that are causally undetermined.

BRIAN: Exactly, so I don't feel warranted in asserting that *all* events are causally determined.

JOHN: Then why are you so skeptical of the libertarian view? If there might be indeterminacy at the subatomic level, why couldn't there be indeterminacy in other parts of the universe? Most importantly, why couldn't there be some causal indeterminacy in some of our decisions and actions?

Before Brian can respond, Prof. Ryan approaches their table with his lunch tray in hand.

PROF. RYAN: Hi, gentlemen. Mind if I join you?

JOHN: Please do.

Prof. Ryan takes a seat with them.

JOHN: Do you know my friend Brian? He's a chemistry major here.

PROF. RYAN: Hi. Bill Ryan. (*He extends his hand to Brian and they shake.*) I don't believe we've met before.

BRIAN: Pleased to meet you.

JOHN (*smiling*): Brian was just about to tell me why you are full of it.

PROF. RYAN (*smiling*): Well, worse things have been said about me, and some of them might be true. Do tell.

JOHN: I told Brian you endorse the libertarian theory of free will. Then I explained the view, and now he's saying the view is not intellectually respectable.

PROF. RYAN: Oh, really?

JOHN: But he's not a determinist.

PROF. RYAN: I see. Well, Brian, why are you so down on my view?

BRIAN: The libertarian view just doesn't sit well with our experiences in general nor does it sit well with a scientific worldview.

PROF. RYAN: Yes, go on.

BRIAN: Well, John and I agree that at the subatomic level of reality there may be some causal indeterminacy in the universe. But, as I see it, there's good reason to think that all phenomena involving objects larger than subatomic particles are determined.

PROF. RYAN: Yes, I see. You espouse what could be called "macro-level determinism."

BRIAN: Yes, and as I said, macro-level determinism is supported by common experience.

You see, we know about the causally determining conditions of many, many phenomena. We also know that often when we don't know the determining conditions for some phenomena, we find them after scientific investigation. Given these facts we have good reason to believe that all macro-level phenomena, including human decisions, are causally determined. Thus, we have good reason to reject the libertarian view of human freedom.

PROF. RYAN: Hmm . . . I don't think that's a very convincing argument.

BRIAN: Why not?

PROF. RYAN: First of all, although there are many phenomena for which we do have perfectly good deterministic explanations, there are also many for which we don't. For instance, suppose my dog has 123,476 hairs on her body. Why are there that many as opposed to 123,479 or 123,326, etc.? Or suppose John here runs a 400-meter dash and finishes in 53.06 seconds. Why does he finish at that time as opposed to 53.07 seconds? Or, in choosing a dessert moments ago, I was torn between the brownies and the pudding. Why did I choose the brownie?

I could go on here, but the point is that there's a heck of a lot that goes on in the world for which we have no deterministic explanation.

BRIAN: Yes, but still when we go looking for the deterministic explanations for such phenomena we often find them. Thus, we still have good reason to believe that all macro level, as opposed to subatomic, events are determined.

PROF. RYAN: Well, admittedly, when we go looking for deterministic explanations that we do not yet possess, we often find them. But we often don't find them either. Consider that in the medical field research has been done to find the causes of cancer and other maladies for years, and although some progress has been made, there's still a hell of a lot that we don't know.

In addition, were scientists to try and figure out the deterministic causes for some of the phenomena mentioned moments ago—such as why my dog has the precise number of hairs she has—they would be hard pressed to ever discover them.

BRIAN: Well played, Dr. Ryan. You make some good points here. But still we find a lot of regularity in the natural world. It seems to me that our best explanation for the regularity in nature and for the success of science in being able to predict the behavior of objects in the natural world requires assuming the truth of macro-level determinism. Thus, we have good reason to believe in macro-level determinism and, consequently, that the libertarian conception of free will must be mistaken.

PROF. RYAN: I'm unconvinced by this line of argument as well. The existence of some macro-level indeterminism is perfectly consistent with the success of science and the observed regularities in nature.

Now, admittedly, indeterminism is not consistent with *complete* regularity in nature, but there's no good reason to think there's complete regularity in nature.

BRIAN: But doesn't the success of science suggest there is complete regularity in nature, at least at the macro level?

PROF. RYAN: No. Successful science involves giving accurate causal accounts of observed phenomena. If the world were completely regular, then I suppose all scientific explanations should be deterministic. However, even if the world was *not* completely deterministic, science could still be successful by offering correct causally deterministic explanations for the perfectly regular phenomena and by offering statistical causal laws to explain phenomena that are not completely regular.

You are aware, aren't you, that not all scientific explanations are deterministic explanations? Rather, sometimes we simply say that given the occurrences of one kind of event there's a, say, eighty percent chance that a certain other event will follow.

JOHN: Yeah, like when the weatherman makes a forecast.

PROF. RYAN: That's right, John, but these sorts of statistical causal explanations don't occur only in meteorology. The health sciences are rife with them as well. Not everyone that smokes will get lung cancer. Smoking just increases the likelihood.

BRIAN: You're right, Dr. Ryan. You can find such statistical causal accounts in all of the natural sciences. But in the sciences we just appeal to these statistical explanations, because we are ignorant of all the factors involved. If we knew all of the relevant factors, we'd be able to give deterministic causal explanations for all macro-level phenomena.

PROF. RYAN: That begs the question, Brian. You are assuming that if we knew all the factors, then we'd find that all macro-level phenomena act deterministically. But this is precisely the point that needs proof here, and you haven't really given any.

BRIAN: I suppose not. But you haven't really given any proof that there is macro-level indeterminism.

PROF. RYAN: That's right, I haven't. But that's because you put forward the view that macro-level determinism is true. I'm simply arguing there's no good reason to think this is correct. I don't need evidence for indeterminism to show there's no good reason to endorse determinism. It might be that given the evidence we should remain agnostic on whether there is any macro-level indeterminism.

BRIAN: Well, maybe I'll think about this, but I doubt it. I prefer to spend my time exploring empirical scientific hypotheses.

Speaking of which, I've got to run to my chem lab. See you later, John. It was nice meeting you, Dr. Ryan.

Brian exits.

JOHN: Do you think we made any headway with him?

PROF. RYAN: I don't know. Some folks are as dogmatic and close minded in their beliefs in determinism as some others are in their religious beliefs.

Marcia Gonzalez, a psychology professor, approaches their table along with one of her students, Rebecca Griffin.

PROF. GONZALEZ: Hi, Bill. Mind if we join you?

PROF. RYAN: I'd be delighted. Have a seat. Who's your friend?

PROF. GONZALEZ: This is Rebecca Griffin. She's one of our psychology majors.

REBECCA: Hi, Dr. Ryan. Pleased to meet you. I've heard a lot about you from other students.

PROF. RYAN: All good reports, I hope.

PROF. GONZALEZ: John, why are you hanging around with this old codger? Are you a philosophy major?

JOHN: Yes, I am.

PROF. GONZALEZ (*to Prof. Ryan*): Plucking the superior fruit out of the garden of minds again, I see.

JOHN: What?

PROF. RYAN: She's just jealous that we draw a lot of the best students into the philosophy program here.

PROF. GONZALEZ: So what's the topic today?

PROF. RYAN: Free will.

PROF. GONZALEZ: Hmm . . . yes. Well, as you know, Bill, I'm often led to wonder about this myself. One can't help it in the field of psychology. You seem to come right up against it.

PROF. RYAN: Of course.

REBECCA: You know, I agree with you guys. The study of psychology does get you thinking about free will, and I'm pretty much convinced that, given the findings of contemporary neuroscientists and psychologists, there is no free will.

PROF. GONZALEZ: Why do you say that?

REBECCA: Well, human decisions and behavior are caused by neural events in the brain, and neuroscientists understand the occurrence of neural events in terms of deterministic causation. So it stands to reason that all human decisions and behavior are deterministically caused.

PROF. RYAN: And I assume your view is that if all human decisions and behavior are deterministically caused then none of them can be free.

REBECCA: Well, yes, of course.

PROF. RYAN: There are a good many philosophers who think free-willed actions may be causally determined. So you'd actually have to do more to prove there's no free will.

REBECCA: Do you think free will is compatible with determinism?

PROF. RYAN: Well . . . no.

REBECCA: So you agree with my argument, then?

PROF. RYAN: No, I don't. Even if I were to grant that freedom is not compatible with determinism, I still wouldn't find your argument convincing.

PROF. GONZALEZ: Me neither.

REBECCA: Really? I'm surprised to hear that from a psychology professor.

PROF. GONZALEZ: Rebecca, a key premise of your argument is false. It's not true that current neuroscience understands the occurrence of all neural events deterministically. Rather, current neuroscience understands various neural processes, such as synaptic transmissions and spike firings, probabilistically.

REBECCA: Oh . . . but couldn't it be that certain neural processes are understood as undetermined only because we don't yet understand all of the factors at work?

  In other words, couldn't, say, spike firings all be determined, but we don't treat them this way in our understanding due to limited background knowledge?

PROF. GONZALEZ: Sure, they *could* all be determined. But that's the point. We don't have any good reason to believe that they *are* all determined. That's why your argument against free will doesn't work.

PROF. RYAN: That and you don't consider the possibility that free will might be compatible with determinism.

REBECCA: Boy, just when you think you've got it all figured out.

PROF. GONZALEZ (*smiling*): Rebecca, I used to think I had it all figured out, too. As you look at things more deeply in the next few years, you'll see that more knowledge just leads to more questions.

Professor Gonzalez pauses and then continues talking.

PROF. GONZALEZ: So, Bill, you reject compatibilist views of free will. I'm a little surprised by that. I thought most philosophers today embraced compatibilist views.

PROF. RYAN: You're right, most do, but there's still a good number of us who favor the libertarian view, and then, of course, there are the free-will skeptics who think there is no free will at all.

PROF. GONZALEZ: You're not in camp with the latter, I take it.

PROF. RYAN: That's right. I side with the libertarians.

PROF. GONZALEZ: It sounds rather old school to me.

PROF. RYAN: I suppose that in one sense that's true. But you might be surprised to know that there are a lot of different contemporary defenses of the libertarian view, and some of them try to uphold the view on grounds that cohere with a naturalistic/scientific worldview. No appeals to non-physical minds acting outside the realm of scientific laws are needed.

PROF. GONZALEZ: I *am* surprised. And you have sympathy with these brands of naturalistic libertarianism?

PROF. RYAN: Sure. I'm especially interested in the ideas of a contemporary thinker named Robert Kane. He says that a lot of our free actions are causally determined by our beliefs and desires—by our character. But these determined free acts are only free insofar as they proceed from a character shaped by prior undetermined free decisions. Kane calls these self-forming acts or SFAs. These occur in situations where we are torn in our decisions between two different things, each of which we are strongly motivated to do.

PROF. GONZALEZ: I see. And does he talk about what the possible neural basis of such undetermined free decisions might be?

PROF. RYAN: As a matter of fact he does. Admittedly, it's fairly speculative stuff. It involves a blending of ideas from quantum physics and chaos theory. In chaotic physical systems very small changes in initial conditions can lead to large and unpredictable changes in the system's subsequent behavior. There is limited scientific data suggesting that under certain conditions chaotic states in the neurons of our brains may allow for the magnification of quantum-level indeterminacies in brain functioning.

PROF. GONZALEZ: I see. So, you—or Kane rather—thinks that in these SFAs chaotic states in the neuronal functioning of our brain may allow for the magnification of quantum-level indeterminacies. In this way, we can make causally undetermined decisions in these contexts of dilemmatic choice.

PROF. RYAN: That's right.

PROF. GONZALEZ: Hmm . . . I'm skeptical, Bill.

PROF. RYAN: Why's that?

PROF. GONZALEZ: Well, in the 1990s a couple of scientists—Roger Penrose and Stuart Hameroff—advocated a related view in which they suggested free-willed decision making could be the result of the magnification of quantum-level indeterminacies in neural processes. However, their view has been subjected to significant criticism by Max Tegmark, a physicist at MIT.

PROF. RYAN: Yes, I'm familiar with Tegmark's work. He argues that the way in which Penrose and Hameroff envision quantum-level indeterminacy effecting human decision making is implausible. He thinks the material conditions of our neurons make the Penrose-Hameroff view of quantum magnification implausible.

PROF. GONZALEZ: Yes, what's the phrase? Oh, yes, the neurons of our brains are "too massive, hot, and wet" for the quantum indeterminacies to have an effect on human decision making.

PROF. RYAN: Yes, that's the phrase. But, Marcia, even if Tegmark is right about the Penrose-Hameroff view on how quantum-level indeterminacies could be magnified so as to allow for causally undetermined decision making, it does not follow that there are no other models of how this might happen.

In a recent book, *Free Will as an Open Scientific Problem*, Mark Balaguer makes this very point, and he even proposes a model of how quantum indeterminacies might be magnified in human decision making, arguing that this model is consistent with Tegmark's views. He also notes that Tegmark himself seems to remain open to the possibility that quantum indeterminacies in the brain are relevant to mental processes.

Balaguer thinks the question of whether libertarian free will exists hangs on whether there are any human decisions that are causally undetermined in the right sort of way, and he thinks this question hangs on whether there can be the right sort of magnification of quantum indeterminacies in brain functioning. He argues that it's a completely open empirical question whether the relevant indeterminacies exist and get amplified in human decision making.

PROF. GONZALEZ: Bill, I must say I remain skeptical. *But* I have to admit to this possibility. Neuroscience is such a new field and there is so much that we don't know right now that it remains possible that some human decisions are causally undetermined.

There's a pause in the conversation. Then Prof. Gonzalez continues.

PROF. GONZALEZ: Bill, have any thoughts on Benjamin Libet's work?

PROF. RYAN: Yes. I don't see his work as having the grave implications for free will that many people seem to think it has.

JOHN: Who's Benjamin Libet?

REBECCA: He was a physiologist who taught at the University of California-San Francisco. He conducted some really interesting experiments, which seem to have implications for human free will.
We read about his experiments in one of my psych classes.

PROF. GONZALEZ: Yes, back in the 1960s it was discovered by neuroscientists that voluntary decisions are preceded in the brain by as much as a second by a slow change in electrical potential. It's called "the readiness potential," and it can be detected by placing sensors on the scalps of experimental subjects. Presumably, occurrence of the readiness potential begins the process of intentional action.

In more recent experiments, Benjamin Libet has shown that the readiness potential occurs 350 to 400 milliseconds prior to conscious awareness of the intention to act and about 550 milliseconds prior to action. In the experiments, human subjects were asked to voluntarily flex their wrists within a certain time interval, and it was found that the readiness potential to engage in these voluntary flexings of the wrist are formed prior to conscious awareness of forming the intention to flex.

The worry for free will here is that these findings suggest that in our voluntary behavior the formation of the intention to act occurs before we are consciously aware of it. If so, it looks as though our voluntary decisions are driven by nonconscious neural processes occurring prior to our conscious awareness. This raises concerns about the extent to which we exert conscious control over our voluntary behavior. Thus, the findings seem to pose a threat to free will.

JOHN: Wow, really?

PROF. RYAN: Oh yes. But it's important not to overestimate what these findings suggest.

PROF. GONZALEZ: Yes, even Dr. Libet felt his findings were consistent with free will having a limited role to play in our voluntary behavior. Notice that I said the readiness potential occurs about 550 milliseconds prior to action and 350 to 400 milliseconds prior to conscious awareness of the intention to act. According to Libet, this means there is about a 150- to 200-millisecond window of opportunity in which we may freely decide to veto our intention to act and do something else.

JOHN: That doesn't sound very reassuring. I like to think that in at least some of my voluntary behavior I freely, consciously, and intentionally choose what I am going to do and then do it. However, if I understand Libet's view correctly, then the formation of the intention to act occurs as a result of neurological processes occurring prior to my conscious awareness, and the only role left for free will is a mere power of veto once the intention is already nonconsciously formed.

PROF. GONZALEZ: Maybe it's the most freedom we can reasonably hope for.

PROF. RYAN: Maybe, but I doubt it. I don't think Libet's findings justify such a limited view of the nature of human free will.

The problem is that, one, Libet's experiments have been conducted in the context of making relatively trivial decisions concerning whether to flex one's wrist or not, and two, we don't really know what the function of the readiness potential is. On my preferred view of free will, the Kanean view, we make causally undetermined free decisions in contexts where we are strongly motivated to do two things and we cannot do both. These are not trivial decisions like Libet's wrist flexings.

Since we don't know what the function of the readiness potential is, then even if it occurs in the more vexing decisions of Kanean self-forming acts, we don't know what it does. In Balaguer's book he gives different accounts of what the readiness potential might be doing in the contexts of decisions like self-forming acts—which he calls "torn decisions"—and none of them suggest that the readiness potential would be a threat to the freedom of such decisions. For instance, in self-forming acts the readiness potential might just be the start of a process leading to the occurrence of such a vexing, or torn, decision, but it might play no role in determining which choice gets made. Thus, the decision made in such a situation may remain wholly un-determined.

For these sorts of reasons, I don't see Libet's work as posing a significant threat to the existence of libertarian free will. Its existence remains an open empirical question. I would note as well that Balaguer is not the only one who has shown that Libet's findings are not as great a threat to free will as some might think. If you're interested, you might also look at Alfred Mele's *Free Will and Luck*, Chapter Two. Mele has other published work on the subject of science and free will that you might want to look at, too.

PROF. GONZALEZ: Those are good points, Bill. I've often felt that Libet's findings were not as conclusive on the free will issue as some think. What you've said gives me a better way to think about what the problem might be. I might want to look up some of those works you mentioned. The problem is finding the time. Gotta run my lab, you know.

You philosophers are fortunate not to be tied down with running labs and experiments. It leaves you free to reflect on what the implications of the scientific findings are for some of life's big questions.

PROF. RYAN: You're right. That's why I chose philosophy. As an under-grad, I majored in psychology and philosophy, and I knew all along I wanted to do graduate work. When it came time to decide I chose philosophy in part because I hated being cooped up in a lab. But I also found the philosophical questions more interesting.

PROF. GONZALEZ: Ever regret choosing the path of philosophy?

PROF. RYAN: Nope. What about you and your path?

PROF. GONZALEZ: No, no regrets here either. I liked philosophy as an undergrad, but I always felt that my answers to the big questions of life stood on such shaky ground. It was too unsettling for me. So I headed to the lab where the questions are smaller but more clearly and easily answerable.

REBECCA: I must say I've enjoyed this conversation very much, but Professor Gonzalez, I'm a bit shocked that you aren't more committed to a deterministic understanding of human behavior. As a professional psychologist working in the field, I should think you'd be more committed to such a perspective.

PROF. GONZALEZ: Rebecca, I approach most of my work with my determinist hat on. That is, as a practicing empirical psychologist, I generally assume that there are deterministic causes at work in human and animal behavior, and I go looking for them. But that's just a working hypothesis upon which I conduct my research. In my more reflective moments—knowing how young experimental psychology and neuroscience are and how little we actually know at this point—I remain much more open-minded on the questions of determinism and human freedom.

REBECCA: Well, I'm still skeptical about human free will.

PROF. GONZALEZ: I am too, but I don't think there's sufficient empirical evidence to rule out the possibility that some of our actions and decisions may be causally undetermined free behaviors.

REBECCA: You know, a lot of our discussion has focused on neuroscientific data. What about the psychological data that suggests there's no free will?

And, Dr. Ryan, you've spent a lot of time today defending libertarian free will against threats from empirical science. But are there any empirical findings suggesting that some human decisions might be causally undetermined free decisions? If not, then your preference for the libertarian conception of free will seems unfounded.

PROF. GONZALEZ: Rebecca, regarding the relevant psychological data, what do you have in mind?

REBECCA: What about the work of Velmans and Wegner, who've shown that conscious awareness of various human decisions and other mental processes lag behind these decisions and processes themselves? Or the work of Festinger, who's shown that people are often mistaken about their reasons for action and even make up reasons for their actions when those aren't the reasons? And what about the work of Stanley Milgram and Isen and Levin, who've shown the significant role of situational factors in determining human behavior?

All of this research raises significant doubt about the existence of human free will, doesn't it?

PROF. GONZALEZ: I think this work may raise some doubts about the *range* of human free will, but I don't think it does anything to challenge the *existence* of free will. That is, although these findings do not show there is no free will, they do perhaps show that not as much of our behavior is a product of free will as we might have initially thought.

Right, Dr. Ryan?

PROF. RYAN: Yes, that's right.

JOHN: Why? I mean, why aren't these findings in empirical psychology a threat to the existence of free will?

REBECCA: Yeah, why?

PROF. GONZALEZ: Bill?

PROF. RYAN: I'll defer to the psychologist here.

PROF. GONZALEZ: If you insist.

First of all, given the kind of phenomena studied by Velmans and Wegner, it's not surprising that they find human consciousness lags behind the mental processes they examine. I mean, of course, we are not consciously aware of all of the things our minds do when processing speech or when instinctively ducking our heads at objects thrown toward us. But just because we are not consciously aware of the mental processes leading to action in these sorts of cases, it does not follow that we *never* have such awareness. For instance, when we make difficult decisions that involve a good bit of reflection, such as choosing a college to attend or a career path, we certainly do seem to be aware of the conscious reasons for our decisions.

I don't think the other research mentioned is a threat to the existence of free will either. You know—the work of Festinger, Milgram, and Isen and Levin. First, too many of the behaviors they examine are not preceded by conscious decisions. It is not surprising to find that a lot of these behaviors in which we don't consciously contemplate what we should do are behaviors the reasons for which we lack knowledge or that are determined by situational factors. Indeed, there may well be adaptive reasons for this. But notice that Dr. Ryan says we exhibit libertarian free will in cases where we have to consciously deliberate about what we should do. So a lot of this research is not relevant to the question of whether we exhibit free will in behavior preceded by conscious decision making.

Having said this, however, their research does suggest that sometimes even our conscious deliberations are significantly influenced by non-conscious factors.

REBECCA: Right, and if our conscious deliberations are influenced by nonconscious factors, then we don't have the kind of control over them for them to be rightly described as "free willed." So there is no free will.

JOHN: Wait a minute. Professor Gonzalez said that the evidence only suggests that *sometimes* our conscious decisions are influenced by nonconscious factors. This leaves open the possibility that in some of our conscious decisions nonconscious factors are inoperative or, at least, so minimal as to be irrelevant. So there's still room for the existence of free will. Right, Professor Gonzalez?

PROF. GONZALEZ: That's right, John.

PROF. RYAN: I couldn't have said it better myself, Marcia.

REBECCA: Fair enough. I suppose even this psychological data doesn't rule out the prospects for free will. But still I'm not sure we should believe in libertarian free will unless there is some kind of empirical evidence for it.

Dr. Ryan, a moment ago I asked if there was any scientific evidence supporting the libertarian view. Is there?

PROF. RYAN: There is some but not much, and there is hardly any kind of consensus in the scientific community regarding the existence of free will. For some of the literature supporting something like libertarian free will, you should consider the work of Martin Heisenberg, an emeritus professor of genetics and neurobiology at the University of Wurzburg, and the work of Bjorn Brembs, a neurobiologist at the Freie Universität in Berlin. The former recently published a paper in *Nature*, and the latter published a relevant piece in *The Proceedings of the Royal Society*. These are both respected scientific journals.

They both argue that our world is not even deterministic at the macro level, and they defend the view that it is not unrealistic to think quantum indeterminacies in brain processes could be magnified in behavior. They've both studied what are adaptive but apparently undetermined behaviors in invertebrates. They think free will could involve a meshing of deterministic with indeterministic neural processes in the brain, and they view this as something that could well have evolved as a consequence of advantages conferred upon variable, nonprogrammed behaviors.

Their view is very interesting, and although it is a minority view in the scientific community, it has able defenders, like themselves. For a very different perspective on the subject you could look at a recent publication by Anthony Cashmore, a biologist at the University of Pennsylvania, who argues that contemporary science points clearly to the conclusion that there is no free will. The relevant piece by Cashmore appeared in another respected journal, *The Proceedings of the National Academy of Sciences*. The article I mentioned earlier by Brembs is to some extent a response to Cashmore's article.

REBECCA: I see. So I suppose the existence of libertarian free will really *is* an open empirical question.

Rebecca pauses and then continues.

REBECCA: Dr. Ryan, one thing you said earlier still bothers me.

PROF. RYAN: Yes, what's that?

REBECCA: You said your preferred view on free will is the libertarian view, which says that some of our free-willed acts must be causally undetermined. If there's no convincing scientific evidence for this view, then why is it your preferred view?

PROF. RYAN: Rebecca, keep in mind that I'm not claiming to know we have libertarian free will. Maybe we do, maybe we don't. As Professor Gonzalez and I have argued here today, its existence would seem to be an open question.

At the same time, and as you rightly note, libertarianism is my preferred view on free will, and I prefer it for philosophical reasons. I believe people are morally responsible for many of their acts and decisions, and for philosophical reasons I don't think we can make sense of moral responsibility unless some of our free-willed acts are causally undetermined. John and I discussed these philosophical issues just a few days ago with my colleagues in the philosophy department.

Furthermore, I think the human capacity for moral responsibility gives human beings a special dignity and worth that is fundamental to a proper system of morality grounded on the concept of respect for persons. For these reasons then the libertarian view of free will is my preferred view. Do we have such free will? Who knows. Maybe in time we'll find out.

REBECCA: Maybe I should take a philosophy class.

PROF. RYAN: We'd love to have you. We're always on the lookout for good, inquiring minds.

PROF. GONZALEZ: Rebecca, you probably should take a course with Bill. Just don't get hooked on the subject.

PROF. RYAN (*smiling*): There are worse ways to spend one's time.

PROF. GONZALEZ (*smiling*): No doubt you've tried some worse ones.

PROF. RYAN: What can I say, I support "experiments in living."

Professor Gonzalez prepares to leave, and Rebecca does the same.

PROF. GONZALEZ: Bill, always a pleasure. Rebecca and I have to head to lab. Let's get together again soon.

PROF. RYAN: Gladly. See you, Marcia.

Prof. Gonzalez and Rebecca exit.

PROF. RYAN: And then there were two.

JOHN: Afraid not, Dr. Ryan. I've got a paper to write.

PROF. RYAN: Well, that's a shame. But you better hit the books. See you.

JOHN: Bye.

> *John exits, leaving Prof. Ryan sitting in an empty cafeteria with his dessert and coffee.*

Study Questions

1. Explain the difference between determinism and macro-level determinism. Why do John and Brian reject determinism? Explain the arguments Brian makes for macro-level determinism, and explain Prof. Ryan's replies to these arguments.

2. Rebecca argues there is no free will. What's her argument? Explain the replies given by Prof. Ryan and Prof. Gonzalez.

3. According to Prof. Ryan, what is the possible neural basis for causally undetermined free decisions? Explain why Prof. Gonzalez thinks Max Tegmark's views undermine Prof. Ryan's account. Explain Prof. Ryan's response to this.

4. Explain the experimental findings of Benjamin Libet and how they are seen as a threat to free will. Explain why Prof. Ryan does not think Libet's findings are as much of a threat to free will as others believe they are.

5. Later in the act, Rebecca says there are psychological, as opposed to neuroscientific, findings that suggest there is no free will. What findings does she cite here? Explain Prof. Gonzalez's reply to this line of argument.

6. Toward the end of the chapter, Rebecca asks Prof. Ryan why the libertarian view of free will is his preferred view if there's no convincing scientific evidence for the view. Explain Prof. Ryan's reply.

Discussion Questions

1. Does Prof. Ryan give good reasons to reject Brian's arguments for macro-level determinism? Explain your answer.

2. Toward the end of the act, Prof. Ryan explains why he prefers the libertarian view of free will even though there's no convincing scientific evidence supporting it. Is his position intellectually respectable? Explain your answer.

3. In this act, both Prof. Ryan and Prof. Gonzalez end up arguing that a libertarian view of free will may be coherent with a scientific worldview. What do you think of this? Does this seem reasonable? Explain your answer.

4. Prof. Gonzalez says that, as a practicing professional psychologist, she works on the assumption that all human behavior is causally determined, but she also says that in her reflective moments she admits to the possibility that some human actions may be causally undetermined free acts. Is she being consistent? Why or why not? Explain.

Suggestions for Further Reading

The ideas in this act have been shaped in significant ways by Chapter 4 of Mark Balaguer's *Free Will as an Open Scientific Problem* (2010). This chapter of his book provides a fine survey of the various scientific arguments, both neuroscientific and psychological, that have been used to challenge the existence of libertarian free will. As noted in Act 4, Balaguer argues in response that the existence of libertarian free will remains an open empirical question. See also Balaguer (2009). Other nice surveys of relevant scientific literature pertaining to free will can be found in the essays by Alfred Mele and Henrik Walter in the *Oxford Handbook of Free Will*, 2nd ed. (2011a). See also Mele (2006, Ch. 2; 2008).

The argument made by Rebecca suggests that there is a kind of "neural determinism" at work in our brains, which suggests there is no libertarian free will. This kind of argument has been made in the literature by Ted Honderich (1988, Ch. 5). See Dayan and Abbott (2001) for information about probabilistic causation in neural functioning. Notice Prof. Ryan tells Rebecca that her neural determinist argument against free will overlooks the possibility that free will may be compatible with determinism. For defenses of such compatibilist views that are informed and supported by scientific findings, see Walter (2001), Flanagan (2002), and Dennett (2003).

Robert Kane has discussed the possible neurological grounds of libertarian free will in several publications. See Kane (1996, 2002c, 2007, 2011a,b). The related work by Penrose and Hameroff can be found in Penrose and Hameroff (1995; 1996). Also, see Skarda and Freeman (1987). For Tegmark's critique of the Penrose-Hameroff view, see Tegmark (2000). Also, see Hodgson (2002) for further discussion of these issues. For explanations and discussions of Libet's work, see Libet et al. (1983) and Libet (2002). It is argued in Henrik Walter (2001) and Max Velmans (1991) that Libet's findings raise significant concerns for the prospect of free will. Again, for a different perspective on the significance of Libet's work, see the relevant works by Balaguer and Mele cited above.

In the second half of Act 4, the discussion moves away from neuro-scientific challenges to the existence of libertarian free will, and consideration is given to the psychological challenges. For the argument that conscious awareness of mental processes, including decision making, lags behind our conscious awareness of such, see Max Velmans (1991) and Daniel Wegner (2002); for evidence that people are often mistaken about their motivations in acting, see Festinger (1957); and for evidence that many of our actions are significantly influenced by seemingly unimportant situational factors, see Milgram (1969) and Isen and Levin (1972). The contemporary philosopher Paul Davies discusses Wegner's work at length in building an argument that scientific findings are inconsistent with contemporary compatibilist and libertarian views of free will; see Davies (2009).

Finally, for very recent scientific work supporting the idea that free-willed actions might be causally undetermined acts involving the magnification of quantum indeterminacies in the brain, see Martin Heisenberg (2009) and Bjorn Brembs (2011). For a recent and more pessimistic scientific perspective on the prospects for libertarian free will, see Anthony Cashmore (2010). Brembs' piece is to some extent a response to Cashmore. For other related recent scientific work, see James Miles (2011) and Greene and Cohen (2004).

Act 5: Free Will and Religion

Scene 1

Monday, 3 p.m. Kate knocks on the open office door of the college chaplain, Rev. Marie Donagan.

REV. DONAGAN: Oh, hi, Kate. Good to see you. Please come in and have a seat.

Kate enters and takes a seat on the couch in Rev. Donagan's office.

REV. DONAGAN: Kate, I just poured myself a cup of tea. Would you like some?

KATE: Yes please, but just half a cup with a lot of cream. Your tea is so strong that it leaves me jumpy if I drink too much of it.

REV. DONAGAN: So I've been told.

She fixes Kate a cup of tea and hands it to her along with a sugar bowl.

REV. DONAGAN: Here. You can add your own sugar.
   Kate, long time no see. What's it been, three weeks?

KATE: Yeah, that's about right. Things have gotten hectic in the last half of the semester.

REV. DONAGAN: Still planning on entering seminary the year after next?

KATE: Yes, I think so. But that's kind of what I wanted to talk to you about.

REV. DONAGAN: What's on your mind?

KATE: Remember how I told you about my family situation growing up? You know, how my father moved out when I was fourteen years old.

REV. DONAGAN: Yes, I remember. It seems to me that, given his abusive character, you and your mother and little brothers were better off without him around.

KATE: Yeah, that's probably right. We probably were better off, but it was all pretty horrible. And, despite his being abusive, it still hurt like hell when he left.

REV. DONAGAN: I'm sure. Even when a father has been abusive toward his family, it is common for his children to take it as a loss when he leaves.
   So, what's up, Kate?

KATE: My father's coming to see me.

REV. DONAGAN: I see. And how does this make you feel?

KATE: Pretty bad. Anxious. Sad. Angry.

REV. DONAGAN: Why don't you tell him not to come?

KATE: I tried to, but then he got so emotional on the phone and said he was sorry for everything he had done. I actually started to feel sorry for him.
   He'll be here next week.

REV. DONAGAN: I see. So what are you going to do?

KATE: I don't know. I've got to decide whether I can forgive him.
   But what's worse is being in touch with him has rekindled old doubts I harbored back when he left the family.

REV. DONAGAN: Yes, we've spoken about this. You wondered if there is a God how could he allow for such behavior on your father's part and why does he let such suffering occur?

KATE: I thought I'd put those worries behind me, but hearing from him and knowing he's coming to visit has caused them to resurface.
   Marie, it's odd. Here I want to go to seminary, and yet, I harbor real doubts about the very existence of the being I want to devote my life to serving. Surely you've had your moments of doubt. How do you deal with them, Marie?

REV. DONAGAN: Yes, I've had many moments of doubt. I suspect I always will have them. It's hard not to have these doubts about God's existence or perfection when one remains thoughtful and aware of the depth of suffering that unfolds in this world.
   So how do I deal with them? Two things—prayer and rational reflection.

KATE: I've tried the prayers, and they offer some solace. But the rational reflections aren't helping much. It's just so hard for me to reconcile God's existence as a perfect, loving, omniscient being with the suffering that occurs in this world.

REV. DONAGAN: Kate, you are, indeed, ever the philosopher.

KATE: Where do you stand on this problem?

REV. DONAGAN: I'm happy to share my views on this with you, Kate, but keep in mind that whatever I say here is just one person's perspective. Different faith traditions will approach this issue differently, and one can find a diversity of perspectives on these matters even within the Christian tradition.

KATE: Yes, I understand. But I'm still curious about your thoughts on this.

REV. DONAGAN: Well, first of all, I believe in the power of free will—a contested issue in the Christian tradition, by the way—and I think the idea of free will can help here. I mean, look, human beings have the freedom to choose whether they will act well or poorly, whether they will treat others appropriately or not, and so on. It's up to us. God has granted us such freedom. What we do with it is up to us. So, if your father has acted like a jerk, this is not God's fault. The bad actions and choices of human beings is no sign of failure on God's part.

KATE: But, Marie, when God granted human beings free will, he surely must have known that some of us would use it to bring great suffering upon us. Thus, our having free will doesn't seem to get God off the hook here. That is, God remains responsible for the suffering in this world.

REV. DONAGAN: Kate, there's more to the story than this. Moral goodness is a special higher order good without which the value of our world would be seriously diminished. True moral goodness involves the performance of noble acts through freedom of choice. Such freedom of choice on the part of human beings allows for some rotten human behavior, but without this freedom our world would be devoid of moral goodness. And, again, without moral goodness the value of our world would be seriously diminished.

KATE: So what you're saying is that we have to have some rotten behavior, like that of my father, if this world is to be a fully good world wherein the higher order value of moral goodness resides.

REV. DONAGAN: That's right, Kate.

KATE: I find this unconvincing.

REV. DONAGAN (smiling): Oh, what have these philosophy professors done to you?

KATE: Don't you see that there are many, many possible worlds God could have created? Logical space is vast. Among these many possible worlds God could have created is a world wherein people have the freedom to choose what they are going to do, but they always happen to choose the right actions. Since a world in which everyone always freely chooses to act rightly is better than a world in which they sometimes freely choose to act wrongly, and since God failed to choose such a world, it would seem that either God does not exist or if he does exist then he is less than perfect.

REV. DONAGAN: Kate, I don't buy that argument. Any world where everyone always chooses to act rightly is a world without free will. Any such world would be a place where God would have granted each person a perfectly good moral character and then set them loose to always act rightly. But genuine human freedom involves shaping our own characters through our free choices made in the face of open possibilities.

KATE: But it could be that there is a logically possible world where God does not dictate character, yet each person just happens to always choose rightly even though they could have done otherwise—even though their choices are not necessitated by their characters.

Again, logical space is vast, and within it there is such a logically possible world. Since God did not create such a world, we have reason to believe that either God does not exist or he's less than perfect.

REV. DONAGAN: Maybe we'll just have to agree to disagree about what kinds of worlds are included within logical space.

But there's something else that deserves consideration here.

KATE: What's that?

REV. DONAGAN: There may be good reason for the existence of the hardships and sufferings of this world. I mean, look at it this way: suppose this world was a paradise where everyone always did the right thing and there were no hardships or suffering—no wicked actions, no diseases, no natural disasters, etc.

Any moral goodness in this world would have a diminished value. Part of what gives moral goodness its value is having it and preserving it in the face of adversity. Furthermore, some virtues, such as courage and benevolence, require adversity. Courage requires danger. Benevolence requires people in need. For there to be a moral goodness of significant value there must be hardships in this world and real choices with open possibilities in the face of these hardships.

KATE: I've encountered this view in my philosophy courses. Irenaeus, a second-century Christian thinker, appealed to these sorts of ideas in responding to the problem of evil.

REV. DONAGAN: That's right, and in the latter half of the twentieth century John Hick has appealed to these ideas in his own theological writings on the subject.

KATE: Marie, I have doubts about this Irenaean theodicy. I worry that it suggests God is not all powerful. If God can only provide for true human goodness through allowing adversity and suffering, then it seems God's power is limited. An omnipotent God should be able to provide for true moral goodness among human beings without all the adversity and suffering we see in this world.

REV. DONAGAN: Omnipotence doesn't entail a capacity to do the logically impossible. Maybe it's logically impossible to have true moral goodness without adversity and suffering. Recall how I said you can't have courage without danger and benevolence without the needy.

If I'm right about this, then God's granting us of a free will that is sometimes misused in the face of such adversities is vindicated.

KATE: Perhaps. I'd certainly like to just accept this, but I still have doubts.

Kate and Rev. Donagan sit quietly for a moment.

KATE: You know, it's funny we're talking about the role of free will in relation to the problem of evil. The whole free will question has been on my mind a lot lately.

REV. DONAGAN: How so?

KATE: Well, John and I . . . you know my friend John, don't you?

REV. DONAGAN (*frowning*): Yes, I know him.

Kate notes Rev. Donagan's frown.

KATE: What?

REV. DONAGAN: What's he think about you going to seminary?

KATE: What does that have to do with anything?

REV. DONAGAN: Well, as you were saying, you and Mr. Party Boy have been . . . .

KATE: Yes, well, we've had a lot of discussions lately about free will with our philosophy professors.

REV. DONAGAN: Yes. And?

KATE: Well, I'm pretty firmly committed to the existence of libertarian free will. You know what that means, don't you?

REV. DONAGAN: Yes, dear, I've taken my fair share of philosophy classes, too.

KATE: Anyway, I've been harboring some theological worries concerning the existence of such free will, and I haven't discussed them with John or my philosophy professors.

REV. DONAGAN: I think I know where this is headed, but why don't you tell me yourself.

KATE: If God's all knowing, then he knows everything we're going to do. But if he knows what we're going to do before we do it, then for every act we ever perform and every decision we ever make, there's a truth about what we'll do that pre-exists our acts and decisions. This suggests we never could do otherwise than what we do. In which case, it would seem that if God's all knowing, then there can be no free will.

REV. DONAGAN: I thought you'd say something along these lines. This is called "the problem of divine foreknowledge." It has a long history and many philosophers have wrestled with the problem.

KATE: I know. We discussed the problem in the course I took on medieval philosophy about a year ago. I just haven't explored the problem in any depth outside of that context. The recent discussions I've had with John and our professors have led me to reconsider it. Do you have an answer to this problem?

REV. DONAGAN: Gosh, I haven't thought about this problem in quite a while. I seem to recall believing that some twentieth-century philosophers were on the right track toward a solution. But why don't you bring me up to speed on the medieval solutions.

KATE: I wasn't really comfortable with any of the medieval solutions we considered, but we can talk about them.

We started with the views of St. Augustine. He maintained that God's foreknowledge of what we are going to do does not inhibit our free will in any way, because although he knows what we will do, this does not cause us to do what we do. His knowledge would only be an infringement on our freedom if it somehow caused us to act as we do. But it doesn't cause us to act as we do; rather, we do what we do as a matter of our own will.

REV. DONAGAN: I see, and why doesn't this work for you?

KATE: As I see it, there can be a problem of divine foreknowledge even if God doesn't cause us to act as we do. The point is that for eternity God has known all that will happen in this world, including everything that every one of us does and decides. So, for instance, God has always known that I would choose to come see you today. If so, then for eternity it has been true that I would choose to come see you today. And if that's so, then it seems my choosing to see you was predestined to occur and I could not have done otherwise. So I did not freely choose this. Further, this is the case not just with this decision of mine but with all human decisions and actions.

So, you see, even if God doesn't cause us to act as we do, his divine foreknowledge still poses a threat to the existence of human freedom.

REV. DONAGAN: I see your point, Kate. You know, the issues are coming back to me, and I'm thinking that the problem can be resolved even if we conceive the problem in the terms you just used.

KATE: How so?

REV. DONAGAN: Well, we might continue to think of God as all knowing, but we might say that as an eternal being God is really a being that stands outside of time. If so, then God's being has no past, present, or future. Thus, he doesn't know what you will do before you do it. Rather, God knows all things as though they occur in an eternal present. That is, God knows all things—past, present, and future—as though they are being seen by him in the present moment. Due to the timelessness of God, he doesn't know what you'll do *before* you do it. Rather, as with all his knowledge, he just knows everything you do, not what you *did* or *will* do. His knowledge does not stand in temporal relations to anything we do or say. So it suggests no predestination of any of our choices.

KATE: Your philosophical studies have not let you down, Marie. We talked about this sort of view in our class. Boethius and St. Thomas Aquinas, two other medieval philosophers, held this sort of view.

REV. DONAGAN: Yes, I'm familiar with these figures. But I forgot that this was their take on the problem of divine foreknowledge. I assume you don't like this solution either.

KATE: No, I don't. Even if God stands outside of time, there's still a problem because we typically understand God as having *perfect* knowledge. Thus, God knows with certainty what we'll do. If he knows with such certainty, then we cannot do otherwise. If we were capable of doing otherwise, there would be ground for some doubt in God's mind. Thus, since he has no doubt in his knowledge of what we'll do, that is, since he is certain about what we'll do, we cannot do otherwise.

REV. DONAGAN: Well, you've got a good point there, too. Did you consider other medieval treatments of the problem?

KATE: Yes, we considered the views of William of Ockham and Luis de Molina. Their views on the subject have been taken very seriously over the ages. But their treatments of the issue turned very technical rather quickly, so I'd be hard pressed to discuss their views on the problem in any responsible fashion right now. I do, however, recall being unconvinced by their views.

Say, earlier you mentioned that some twentieth-century thinkers had views on the problem that you find promising. What are these views?

REV. DONAGAN: Have you ever heard of process philosophy?

KATE: No, I can't say that I have.

REV. DONAGAN: It's a school of thought that became fairly prominent in the twentieth century. Two of the leading exponents of the view were Alfred North Whitehead and Charles Hartshorne.

KATE: I've heard of Whitehead. Didn't he coauthor *Principia Mathematica* with Bertrand Russell?

REV. DONAGAN: That's right.

Process philosophy spawned a brand of theology that shares a similar name—"process theology." And process theology espouses "open theism" as a solution to the problem of divine foreknowledge.

KATE: Sounds interesting. What are the details?

REV. DONAGAN: The basic idea is something like this: human beings possess libertarian free will. That is, many of our actions and decisions are causally undetermined and free. We often make decisions where the options before us are genuinely open.

When we act with such freedom God does not know what we are going to do. At best, he knows what we are likely to do in these situations, but he does not know exactly what we will do.

KATE: But God is supposed to be ominiscient—all knowing. Are the open theists simply going to deny the omniscience of God?

REV. DONAGAN: That's one of the really interesting elements of their view. They don't deny the omniscience of God. Omniscience requires knowing all facts and what is logically entailed by those facts. So God knows everything about the past and the present, and he is even able to know facts about the future, which are logically entailed by facts of the past and present. For instance, when God sees a rock tossed off of the Eiffel Tower he knows where it will land given his full knowledge of the laws of nature and the facts surrounding the situation of its being tossed. He is able to foresee this because where the rock lands is causally determined by the natural laws and the conditions at the time of its being tossed.

However, when it comes to causally undetermined events, such as our libertarian free decisions, God does not know what will happen. In these cases, the laws of nature and facts of the past and present do not logically entail what will occur in the future. But this does not mean God lacks omniscience. Omniscience is knowing all the facts and what they logically entail. God knows all of this. So he is omniscient. Causally undetermined future events, such as our future, libertarian-free decisions, have not occurred yet nor are they logically entailed by any facts past or present. Thus, with respect to what we will do in such free actions there are really no facts to be known that shed light on what will transpire. As such, although God lacks foreknowledge in the case of our libertarian-free actions, he remains omniscient.

KATE: Marie, that's really interesting. I'm going to have to look into this further. I can see already that open theism seems to embrace a somewhat unorthodox conception of God.

REV. DONAGAN: Yes, many people feel this way. What's on your mind?

KATE: Well, for one thing, God has traditionally been conceived as an eternal, *unchanging*, perfect being. However, according to this view God's knowledge grows over time. As more and more of the causally undetermined events of this world occur, God comes to know more.

REV. DONAGAN: Good point. Anything else?

KATE: Well, I have at least two more points. First, God has also been traditionally conceived as a being that creates and sustains the world, but he is unaffected by what transpires within it. According to open theism, God *would* be affected by what goes on here, since his knowledge would grow over time in reaction to what we freely decide to do.

Second, in the Bible God is portrayed as capable of foretelling what people are going to do, and he doesn't seem to simply know what they are likely to do. God appears to be certain of what will transpire. So open theism may entail a vision of God that doesn't sit well with scripture.

REV. DONAGAN: Kate, you've certainly located some of the key theological concerns related to the view. I must tell you that despite these unorthodox elements of the view I'm still attracted to it. Like you, I don't find the medieval solutions to be adequate, and in the face of the problem of divine foreknowledge I think it's time for us religious types to start thinking "outside the box."

KATE (*smiling*): Shh . . . you'll be labeled a heretic.

REV. DONAGAN: Ha! Hardly. You know as well as I do that at this institution there's plenty of open and vigorous discussion on the nature of God and his relationship to his creation.

The conversation ends momentarily. There's a pregnant pause. Kate sits looking pensively out the window.

REV. DONAGAN: Kate, what are you going to do?

KATE (*still looking out the window*): Look up some of this process theology and open theism.

REV. DONAGAN: That's not what I mean. Your father—what are you going to do?

KATE: I don't know. He really hurt me, Marie. He hurt the whole family.

There's a moment of silence again. Kate still looks out the window.

KATE: My mother has forgiven him. She always said that he couldn't help being the way he was. She said my father's father acted the same way and eventually deserted my father's family when my dad was a teenager. Mom thinks that without a proper role model growing up my father could not be expected to do otherwise than what he did. So she forgives him.

REV. DONAGAN: What do you think?

KATE: A couple of things. First, that's *not* forgiveness; that's *excusing* him. Second, I think the grounds of her excuse are dubious. The mere fact that my father's father did the same things doesn't mean my father had no proper role models, and it certainly doesn't mean he couldn't have done otherwise.

I think my father was responsible for what he did. Thus, I can't excuse him. I can only forgive him, or not.

REV. DONAGAN: Kate, you are so right. True forgiveness must be given in acknowledgment of the responsibility of the other. Otherwise, it becomes excuse. This is why true forgiveness can be so hard.

Kate stands and gathers her things.

KATE: Marie, I gotta go. I need to sort through this.

As she reaches the doorway, she turns to Rev. Donagan.

KATE: Thanks, Marie.

REV. DONAGAN: Anytime.

Scene 2

Monday, 4:20 p.m. John and the other members of the judicial board are in the middle of deliberation about whether Janet Richardson should be expelled for plagiarism.

JENNY: Look, I know plagiarism, especially the kind that Janet has engaged in, is a very serious offense, and I know that she has admitted to her own guilt and that she knew what she was doing was wrong. However, consider her life circumstances.

Remember she said she comes from a culture of cheating in her high school, and perhaps more important, she is under tremendous pressure from her parents to do well and she is struggling to maintain her scholarship. Given these facts it's no wonder she's been cheating here at college. I'm not sure she could be reasonably expected to do otherwise. Thus, I don't think she merits our harshest punishment.

ARMANDO: As I said earlier, she should be expelled.

JENNY: But that *is* our harshest punishment.

ARMANDO: I know, but hers is an obvious and egregious case of plagiarism. If we don't expel her for plagiarism, then no one should be expelled for it.

JENNY: That's not true. Others might deserve expulsion, but as I just got done saying, her circumstances are special, diminishing her responsibility for what she has done. Thus, I don't think she deserves expulsion.

ARMANDO: Yes, but I disagree with your argument. A lot of people face situations just like hers and they don't cheat. For instance, a lot of people go to high schools where cheating is rampant while also facing tremendous pressure to do well, yet they still don't cheat. Thus, I don't think the conditions she faced indicate that she couldn't have done otherwise.

JENNY: But maybe not all humans are wired the same way. Perhaps some people are more naturally inclined to cave in to the impulse to cheat than others and that's why humans will respond differently when facing similar pressures.

Armando, although you and I might not cheat when facing the same pressures as Janet, maybe she is put together in such a way so that she is bound to cheat.

ARMANDO: But we don't know that.

JENNY: We don't know that she isn't either. That's why I oppose expulsion.

ARMANDO: I still disagree. Using that logic, it seems to me that no one would ever deserve punishment for anything, because for all we know we might *all* be victims of genetic and environmental factors robbing us of ultimate responsibility for any and all of our actions.

JENNY: Ugh . . . I don't think we're getting anywhere here.

ARMANDO: Me neither. I'm afraid we're just not going to come to agreement on this case.

JENNY: Yes, it's too bad.

While Armando and Jenny have been debating the issue, John has been listening and staring out the window immersed in thought.

ARMANDO: John, it looks like you've got the deciding vote here on the expulsion question. What's it going to be?

John briefly chuckles and shakes his head while still looking out the window.

JOHN (*still looking out the window, mutters to himself*): So, now the question of responsibility becomes *my* responsibility.

ARMANDO AND JENNY: What?

JOHN (*turning to them*): Nothing, you wouldn't believe the week I've had.

THE END

Study Questions

1. Kate explains the basis for her doubts about the existence of a perfect, loving, omniscient God. What is the basis for her doubt?

2. Explain the role the concept of free will plays in Rev. Donagan's attempt to quell Kate's doubts about God's existence, and explain the criticism Kate makes of Rev. Donagan's "free will" defense.

3. Explain the basic idea behind the Irenaean theodicy, which is considered in this act.

4. Explain the problem of divine foreknowledge.

5. How did St. Augustine try to solve the problem of divine foreknowledge? Explain the criticism Kate provides of this Augustinian solution.

6. How did Boethius and Aquinas try to solve the problem of divine foreknowledge? Explain the criticism Kate provides of their solution.

7. How is the open theism of process theology intended to solve the problem of divine foreknowledge? Explain the reasons Kate gives for saying open theism seems to provide an unorthodox view of the nature of God.

8. Explain the distinction between forgiveness and excuse, which is made toward the end of this act.

Discussion Questions

1. Does the existence of human free will help in solving the problem of evil? Why or why not? Explain your answer.

2. Does the Irenaean theodicy solve the problem of evil? Why or why not? Explain your answer.

3. In this act, two medieval solutions to the problem of divine foreknowledge are discussed and Kate rejects both of them. Does she give good reasons to reject them? Why or why not? Explain your answer.

4. Does open theism offer a good solution to the problem of divine foreknowledge? Why or why not? Explain your answer.

5. What do you think of Rev. Donagan's claim that "True forgiveness must be given in acknowledgment of the responsibility of the other. Otherwise, it becomes excuse"? Is this true? Explain your answer.

6. At the end of the dialogue, John is faced with the burden of deciding whether Janet should be expelled or receive a lesser punishment. What would you do if you were in John's shoes? Explain your answer, while also developing reactions to the points made by Armando and Jenny.

Suggestions for Further Reading

In the beginning of this act, the problem of evil is considered along with the free-will solution to this problem. A classic twentieth-century discussion of the problem can be found in Mackie (1955). This article has been reprinted in many editions of Joel Feinberg and Russ Shafer-Landau's *Reason and Responsibility*. Mackie critically examines various proposed solutions to the problem of evil, including the free-will solution. A more recent and more technical introduction to the problem of evil can be found in Tooley (2009), which includes a very extensive bibliography.

As mentioned in the text, John Hick is a twentieth-century theologian who has defended the Irenaean response to the problem of evil (see Hick, 1966). Tooley (2009) offers criticism of this Irenaean solution. A more detailed criticism of Hick's Irenaean theodicy can be found in Madden and Hare (1968). The readings by Hick and Madden and Hare can be found in Pojman's *Philosophy of Religion: An Anthology* (1998). For defenses of the free-will solution to the problem of evil, see Plantinga (1974) and Swinburne (1996). A nice excerpt from Swinburne, which covers the relevant matters, can be found in the 13th edition of *Reason and Responsibility*, Feinberg and Shafer-Landau, eds. (2008). A nice excerpt from Plantinga (1974) appears in Pojman (1998). Both Mackie (1955) and Tooley (2009) offer criticism of the free-will solution.

In later stages of this act, the problem of divine foreknowledge is considered. A good introduction to the problem and different proposed solutions to it can be found in Kane (2005, Ch. 13). Other nice introductions for beginners appear in Hasker (2002, 2011). A more technical introduction, which covers the more recent literature on the subject, can be found in Zagzebski (2011). Zagzebski's piece includes a very extensive bibliography on the subject. For some book-length treatments of the subject, see Hasker (1989) and Zagzebski (1991).

St. Augustine's response to the problem of divine foreknowledge can be found in his *On the Free Choice of the Will* (1964). Relevant excerpts from Augustine are included in Pojman (1998) and Kane (2002b). Boethius's proposed solution, which appeals to the timelessness of God, can be found in his *The Consolation of Philosophy*, Bk. V, prose vi (1962). St. Thomas Aquinas takes a similar view. See his *Summa Theologica* Ia, q. 14, art. 13, and the *Summa Contra Gentiles* I, Ch. 66. Some notable contemporary defenses of this view can be found in Stump and Kretzmann (1981, 1991) and Rota (2010). For criticism of this approach, see Pike (1970) and Zagzebski (1991, Ch. 2).

As noted, there are other important medieval treatments of the subject. See Luis de Molina, *On Divine Foreknowledge: Pt. IV of The Concordia* (1988). Also, see William of Ockham, *Predestination, Foreknowledge, and Future Contingents* (1983). For a nice beginners' introduction to these especially subtle views, see Hasker (2002) and Kane (2005, Ch. 13). Both of these medieval views have been given a significant amount of attention in the recent literature. For more on this, see Zagzebski (2011).

Process theology and open theism are considered toward the end of this act. These views are considered in Kane (2005, Ch. 13) and Hasker (2011). For more on these views, see Griffin and Cobb (1976); Pinnock, Rice, Sanders, Hasker, and Basinger (1994); and Viney (2008). For more extensive discussion and defense of open theism, see Hasker (2004) and Sanders (2007).

Bibliography

Amsterdam, A. "Capital Punishment." *Stanford Magazine* (Fall/Winter), 1977.

———. *Summa Theologica*, Ia, q.14, art. 13. Chicago: Encyclopedia Britannica, 1952.

Aquinas, Thomas. *Summa Contra Gentiles*, I, Ch. 66. New York: Hanover House, 1955.

Aristotle. *Nicomachean Ethics*, trans. W.D. Ross. New York: Oxford University Press, 1925.

Augustine, St. *On the Free Choice of the Will*. Indianapolis: Bobbs-Merrill, 1964.

Ayer, A.J. "Freedom and Necessity." In *Philosophical Essays*, 3–20. New York: St. Martin's Press, 1954.

Balaguer, M. "Why There Are No Good Arguments for Any Interesting Version of Determinism." *Synthese* 168 (2009): 1–21.

———. *Free Will as an Open Scientific Problem*. Cambridge, MA: MIT Press, 2010.

Bedau, H. "How to Argue About the Death Penalty." *Israel Law Review* 25 (1991): 466–80.

Bentham, J. *An Introduction to the Principles of Morals and Legislation*, eds. J.H. Burns and H.L.A. Hart. London: Methuen, Inc., 1970. Excerpts reprinted in Gorr and Harwood, 1995, 286–95.

Berkeley, G. (1710). *A Treatise Concerning the Principle of Human Knowledge*, ed. J. Dancy. Oxford: Oxford University Press, 1998.

Bernstein, M. "Kanean Libertarianism." *Southwest Philosophy Review* 11 (1995): 151–57.

Berofsky, B. "Ultimate Responsibility in a Determined World." *Philosophy and Phenomenological Research* 60 (2000): 135–40.

———. "Compatibilism without Frankfurt: Dispositional Analyses of Free Will." In R. Kane, 2011a, 153–74.

Boethius. *The Consolation of Philosophy*. Indanapolis: Bobbs-Merrill, 1962.

Brembs, B. "Towards a Scientific Concept of Free Will as a Biological Trait: Spontaneous Actions and Decision-Making in Invertebrates." *Proceedings of the Royal Society B* 278 (2011): 930–39.

Broad, C.D. *Ethics and the History of Philosophy*. London: Routledge & Kegan Paul, 1952.

Cashmore, A. "The Lucretian Swerve: The Biological Basis of Human Behavior and the Criminal Justice System." *Proceedings of the National Academy of Sciences* 107 (2010): 4499–504.

Chisholm, R.M. "Human Freedom and the Self." The Lindley Lecture. Department of Philosophy, University of Kansas, 1964. Reprinted in R. Kane, 2002b, 47–58.

———. *Person and Object: A Metaphysical Study*. La Salle, IL: Open Court, 1976.

Clarke, R. "Indeterminism and Control." *American Philosophical Quarterly* 32 (1995): 125–38.

———. "Free Choice, Effort, and Wanting More." *Philosophical Explorations* 2 (1999): 20–41.

———. (2002). "Libertarian Views: Critical Survey of Noncausal and Event-Causal Accounts of Free Agency." In R. Kane, 2002a, 356–85.

———. *Libertarian Accounts of Free Will*. New York: Oxford University Press, 2003.

———. "Incompatibilist (Nondeterministic) Theories of Free Will." In *The Stanford Encyclopedia of Philosophy*, ed. E. Zalta, 2008, online edition: http://plato.stanford.edu/entries/incompatibilism-theories.

Davies, P. *Subjects of the World: Darwin's Rhetoric and the Study of Agency in Nature*. Chicago: University of Chicago Press, 2009.

Dayan, P., and Abbott, L.F. *Theoretical Neuroscience*. Cambridge, MA: MIT Press, 2001.

de Molina, L. *On Divine Foreknowledge*, trans. A. Freddoso. Ithaca, NY: Cornell University Press, 1988.

Dennett, D. "On Giving Libertarians What They Say They Want." In *Brainstorms: Philosophical Essays on Mind and Psychology*. Montgomery, VT: Goldfarb Books, 1978.

———. *Elbow Room: The Varieties of Free Will Worth Wanting*. Cambridge, MA: MIT Press, 1984a.

———. "I Could Not Have Done Otherwise—So What?" *Journal of Philosophy* 81 (1984b): 553–56.

———. *Freedom Evolves*. New York: Penguin Books, 2003.

d'Holbach, P. (1770). "The Illusion of Free Will," trans. H.D. Robinson. In J. Feinberg and R. Shafer-Landau, 1999, 416–21.

Double, R. *The Non-Reality of Free Will*. Oxford: Oxford University Press, 1991.

Doyle, B. *Free Will: The Scandal in Philosophy*. Cambridge, MA: I-Phi Press, 2011.

Edwards, P. "Hard and Soft Determinism." In *Determinism and Freedom in the Age of Modern Science*, ed. Sidney Hook. New York: New York University Press, 1958. Reprinted in R. Kane, 2002b, 59–67.

Ekstrom, L. *Free Will: A Philosophical Study*. Boulder: Westview Press, 2000.

———. "Free Will, Chance, and Mystery." *Philosophical Studies* 113 (2003): 153–80.

Fara, M. "Masked Abilities and Compatibilism." *Mind* 117 (2008): 843–65.

Feinberg, J. "The Classic Debate." In J. Feinberg and J. Coleman, 2000, 727–31.

Feinberg, J., and Coleman, J., eds. *Philosophy of Law*, 6th ed. Belmont, CA: Wadsworth, 2000.

Feinberg, J., and Shafer-Landau, R., eds. *Reason and Responsibility: Readings in Some Basic Problems of Philosophy*, 10th ed. Belmont, CA: Wadsworth, 1999.

Festinger, L. *A Theory of Cognitive Dissonance*. Palo Alto, CA: Stanford University Press, 1957.

Fischer, J.M. *The Metaphysics of Free Will: A Study of Control*. New York: Blackwell, 1994.

———. "Recent Work on Moral Responsibility." *Ethics* 110 (1999): 93–139.

———. *My Way: Essays on Moral Responsibility*. New York: Oxford University Press, 2006.

Fischer, J.M., and Ravizza, M., eds. *Perspectives on Moral Responsibility*. Ithaca: Cornell University Press, 1993.

———. *Responsibility and Control: A Theory of Moral Responsibility*. Cambridge, UK: Cambridge University Press, 1998.

Flanagan, O. *The Problem of the Soul: Two Visions of the Mind and How to Reconcile Them*. New York: Basic Books, 2002.

Frankfurt, H. "Alternate Possibilities and Moral Responsibility." *Journal of Philosophy* 66 (1969): 829–39.

———. "Freedom of the Will and the Concept of a Person." *Journal of Philosophy* 68 (1971): 5–20.

Ginet, C. *On Action.* Cambridge, UK: Cambridge University Press, 1990.

———. "In Defense of the Principle of Alternative Possibilities: Why I Don't Find Frankfurt's Argument Convincing." *Philosophical Perspectives* 10 (1996): 403–17.

———. "Freedom, Responsibility, and Agency." *Journal of Ethics* 1 (1997): 85–98.

Goetz, S. "A Noncausal Theory of Agency." *Philosophy and Phenomenological Research* 49 (1988): 303–16.

———. "Libertarian Choice." *Faith Philosophy* 14 (1997): 195–211.

Golding, M. *Philosophy of Law.* Englewood Cliffs, NJ: Prentice-Hall, 1975.

Gorr, M., and Harwood, S., eds. *Crime and Punishment: Philosophic Explorations.* Boston: Jones and Bartlett, 1995.

Greene, J., and Cohen, J. "For the Law, Neuroscience Changes Nothing and Everything." *Philosophical Transactions of the Royal Society B* 359 (2004): 1775–85.

Griffin, D., and Cobb, J. *Process Theology: An Introductory Exposition.* Philadelphia: Westminster Press, 1976.

Griffith, M. "Why Agent-Caused Actions Are Not Lucky." *American Philosophical Quarterly* 47 (2010): 43–56.

Haji, I. "Indeterminism and Frankfurt-type Examples." *Philosophical Explorations* 2 (1999): 42–58.

———. "Active Control, Agent-causation, and Free Action." *Philosophical Explorations* 7 (2004): 131–48.

Hasker, W. *God, Time, and Knowledge.* Ithaca: Cornell University Press, 1989.

———. "God, Time, Knowledge, and Freedom: The Historical Matrix." In R. Kane, 2002b, 264–83.

———. *Providence, Evil, and the Openness of God.* London: Routledge, 2004.

———. "Divine Foreknowledge and Human Freedom." In R. Kane, 2011a, 39–54.

Heisenberg, M. "Is Free Will an Illusion?" *Nature* 459 (2009): 1052–53.

Hick, J. *Evil and the God of Love*. New York: Harper and Row, 1966.

Hobbes, T. *Leviathan*. Indianapolis: Bobbs-Merrill, 1958.

Hodgson, D. "Quantum Physics, Consciousness, and Free Will." In R. Kane, 2002a, 85–110.

———. *Rationality + Consciousness = Free Will*. New York: Oxford University Press, 2012.

Honderich, T. *A Theory of Determinism: The Mind, Neuroscience, and Life-Hopes*. New York: Oxford University Press, 1988.

———. *How Free Are You?* New York: Oxford University Press, 1993.

Hume, D. (1748). *An Enquiry Concerning Human Understanding*. In *The Empiricists*, reprinted in J. Locke, G. Berkeley, and D. Hume. New York: Anchor Books, 1974.

Hunt, D. "Moral Responsibility and Unavoidable Action." *Philosophical Studies* 97 (2000): 195–227.

———. "Moral Responsibility and Buffered Alternatives." *Midwest Studies in Philosophy* 29 (2005): 126–45.

Isen, A., and Levin, P. "Effect of Feeling Good on Helping." *Journal of Personality and Social Psychology* 21 (1972): 384–88.

Kane, R. *Free Will and Values*. Albany, NY: SUNY Press, 1985.

———. *The Significance of Free Will*. New York: Oxford University Press, 1996.

———, ed. *The Oxford Handbook of Free Will*. New York: Oxford University Press, 2002a.

———, ed. *Free Will*. New York: Oxford University Press, 2002b.

———. (2002c). "Some Neglected Pathways in the Free Will Labyrinth." In R. Kane, 2002a, 406–37.

———. *A Contemporary Introduction to Free Will*. New York: Oxford University Press, 2005.

———. "Libertarianism." In *Four Views on Free Will*, eds. J. M. Fischer, R. Kane, D. Pereboom, and M. Vargas, 5–43. Oxford: Blackwell, 2007.

———, ed. *The Oxford Handbook of Free Will*, 2nd ed. New York: Oxford University Press, 2011a.

———. (2011b). "Rethinking Free Will: New Perspectives on an Ancient Problem." In R. Kane, 2011a, 381–404.

Kant, I. (1887). *The Philosophy of Law, Part II* (trans. W. Hastie). Portions reprinted as "The Retributive Theory of Punishment" in J. White, 2012, 212–14.

———. (1788). *Critique of Practical Reason*, trans. L.W. Beck. Indianapolis: Bobbs-Merrill, 1956.

Lemos, J. "Kanian Freedom and the Problem of Luck." *Southern Journal of Philosophy* 45 (2007): 515–32.

———. "Kane's Libertarian Theory and Luck: A Reply to Griffith." *Philosophia* 39 (2011a): 357–67.

———. "Wanting, Willing, and Trying and Kane's Theory of Free Will." *Dialectica* 65 (2011b): 31–48.

Levy, N. "Contrastive Explanations: A Dilemma for Libertarians." *Dialectica* 59 (2005): 51–61.

Libet, B., Gleason, C., Wright, E., and Pearl, D. (2002). "Do We Have Free Will?" In R. Kane, 2002a, 551–64.

———. "Time of Conscious Intention to Act in Relation to Cerebral Potential." *Brain* 106 (1983): 623–42.

Locke, J. (1690). *An Essay Concerning Human Understanding*. In *The Empiricists*. New York: Anchor Books, 1974.

Mackie, J.L. "The Problem of Evil." *Mind* 64 (1955): 200–212.

Madden, E., and Hare, P. *Evil and the Concept of God*. Springfield, IL: Charles C. Thomas Publisher, 1968.

McCann, H. *The Works of Agency: On Human Action, Will, and Freedom*. Ithaca: Cornell University Press, 1998.

McKenna, M. "Compatibilism." In *The Stanford Encyclopedia of Philosophy*, ed. E. Zalta, 2004, online edition: http://plato.Stanford.edu/archives/sum2004/entries/compatibilism/.

Mele, A. *Autonomous Agents: From Self-Control to Autonomy*. New York: Oxford University Press, 1995.

———. "Soft Libertarianism and Frankfurt-Style Scenarios." *Philosophical Topics* 24 (1996): 123–41.

———. "Kane, Luck, and the Significance of Free Will." *Philosophical Explorations* 2 (1999a): 96–104.

———. "Ultimate Responsibility and Dumb Luck." *Social Philosophy and Policy* 16 (1999b): 274–93.

———. "Libertarianism, Luck, and Control." *Pacific Philosophical Quarterly* 86 (2005): 381–407.

———. *Free Will and Luck*. New York: Oxford University Press, 2006.

———. "Recent Work on Free Will and Science." *American Philosophical Quarterly* 45 (2008): 102–29.

———. "Free Will and Science." In R. Kane, 2011a, 499–514.

Mele, A., and Robb, D. "Rescuing Frankfurt-style Cases." *Philosophical Review* 107 (1998): 97–112.

Miles, J. "Irresponsible and a Disservice: The Integrity of Social Psychology Turns on the Free Will Dilemma." *British Journal of Social Psychology* (2011), doi: 10-1111/j2044-8309.2011:02077x.

Milgram, S. *Obedience to Authority*. New York: Harper and Row, 1969.

Mill, J.S. *A System of Logic*. New York: Harper and Row, 1874.

Moore, G.E. "Free Will." In *Ethics*, ed. Moore, 84–95. Oxford: Oxford University Press, 1912.

Moore, M. "The Moral Worth of Retribution." In *Responsibility, Character and the Emotions*, ed. F. Schoeman. Cambridge, UK: Cambridge University Press, 1987. Reprinted in J. Feinberg and J. Coleman, 2000, 746–69.

Nielsen, K. "The Compatibility of Freedom and Determinism." In *Reason and Practice*. New York: Harper and Row, 1971.

Ockham, W. *Predestination, God's Foreknowledge, and Future Contingents*, 2nd ed., trans. M. McCord-Adams and N. Kretzmann. Indianapolis, IN: Hackett, 1983.

O'Connor, T. "Why Agent Causation?" *Philosophical Topics* 24 (1996): 143–58.

———. *Persons and Causes: The Metaphysics of Free Will*. New York: Oxford University Press, 2000.

———. "Agent-causal Power." In *Dispositions and Causes*, ed. T. Hanfield, 189–214. Oxford: Oxford University Press, 2009.

———. "Agent-Causal Theories of Freedom." In R. Kane, 2011a, 309–28.

Penrose, R., and Hameroff, S.R. "What 'Gaps'? Reply to Grush and Churchland." *Journal of Consciousness Studies* 2 (1995): 98–111.

———. "Conscious Events as Orchestrated Space-Time Selections." *Journal of Consciousness Studies* 3 (1996): 36–53.

Pereboom, D. *Living Without Free Will*. Cambridge, UK: Cambridge University Press, 2001.

———. "Hard Incompatibilism." In *Four Views on Free Will*, eds. J.M. Fischer, R. Kane, D. Pereboom, and M. Vargas, 85–125. Oxford:

Blackwell, 2007.

Pereboom, D. *Free Will*. Indiannapolis: Hackett, 2009.

Pike, N. *God and Timelessness*. New York: Schocken Press, 1970.

Pinnock, C., Rice, R., Sanders, J., Hasker, W., and Basinger, D. *The Openness of God*. Downers Grove, IL: Intervarsity Press, 1994.

Plantinga, A. *God, Freedom, and Evil*. New York: Harper and Row, 1974.

Pojman, L. *Philosophy of Religion: An Anthology*, 3rd ed. Belmont, CA: Wadsworth, 1998.

Reid, T. (1788). *Essays on the Active Powers of the Human Mind*. Cambridge, MA: MIT Press, 1969.

Reiman, J. "Against the Death Penalty." In *Living Well*, ed. S. Luper. New York: Houghton Mifflin Harcourt, 1998. Reprinted in J. White, 2012, 220–28.

Rota, M. "The Eternity Solution to the Problem of Human Freedom and Divine Foreknowledge." *European Journal for Philosophy of Religion* 2 (2010): 165–86.

Rowe, W. *Thomas Reid on Freedom and Morality*. Ithaca: Cornell University Press, 1991.

———. "The Metaphysics of Freedom: Reid's Theory of Agent Causation." *American Catholic Philosophical Quarterly* 74 (2000): 425–46.

———. "Free Will, Moral Responsibility, and the Problem of 'Oomph.'" *Journal of Ethics* 10 (2006): 295–313.

Sanders, J. *The God Who Risks: A Theology of Divine Providence*. Downers Grove, IL: Intervarsity Press, 2007.

Shafer-Landau, R. "The Failure of Retributivism." *Philosophical Studies* 82 (1996): 289–316. Reprinted in J. Feinberg and J. Coleman, 2000, 769–79.

Skarda, C., and Freeman, W. "How Brains Make Chaos in Order to Make Sense of the World." *Behavior and Brain Sciences* 10 (1987): 161–95.

Smart, J.J.C. "Free Will, Praise, and Blame." *Mind* 70 (1963): 291–306.

Smilansky, S. *Free Will and Illusion*. Oxford: Clarendon Press, 2000.

Strawson, G. *Freedom and Belief*. New York: Oxford University Press, 1986.

———. "The Unhelpfulness of Indeterminism." *Philosophy and Phenomenological Research* 60 (2000): 149–55.

Stump, E. "Cartesian Dualism and Materialism without Reductionism." *Faith and Philosophy* 12 (1995): 505–31.

———. "Libertarianism Freedom and the Principle of Alternative Possibilities." In *The Evidential Problem of Evil*, ed. D. Howard-Snyder, 73–88. Bloomington: Indiana University Press, 1996.

Stump, E., and Kretzmann, N. "Eternity." *Journal of Philosophy* 78 (1981): 429–58.

———. "Prophecy, Past, and Eternity." *Philosophical Perspectives* 5 (1991): 395–424.

Swinburne, R. *Is There a God?* New York: Oxford University Press, 1996.

Taylor, R. *Action and Purpose*. Englewood Cliffs, NJ: Prentice-Hall, 1966.

———. *Metaphysics*, 4th ed. Englewood Cliffs, NJ: Prentice-Hall, 1992.

Tegmark, M. "The Importance of Quantum Decoherence in Brain Processes." *Physical Review E* 61 (2000): 4194–206.

Tooley, M. (2009). "The Problem of Evil." *Stanford Encyclopedia of Philosophy*, 2009, online edition: http://plato.stanford.edu/entries/evil.

Van den Haag, E. "The Ultimate Punishment: A Defense." *Harvard Law Review* 99 (1986): 1662–69. Reprinted in J. White, 2012, 214–20.

Van Inwagen, P. *An Essay on Free Will*. Oxford: Clarendon Press, 1983.

———. "Free Will Remains a Mystery." In R. Kane, 2002a, 158–77.

Velmans, M. "Is Human Information Processing Conscious?" *Behavioral and Brain Sciences* 14 (1991): 651–69.

Vihvelin, K. "Free Will Demystified: A Dispositional Account." *Philosophical Topics* 32 (2004): 427–50.

Viney, D. "Process Theism." *Stanford Encyclopedia of Philosophy*, 2008, http://plato.stanford.edu/entries/process-theism/.

Waller, B. "Free Will Gone Out of Control." *Behaviorism* 16 (1988): 149–62.

Walter, H. *The Neurophilosophy of Free Will*. Cambridge, MA: MIT Press, 2001.

———. "Contributions of Neuroscience to the Free Will Debate: From Random Movement to Intelligible Action." In R. Kane, 2011a,

515–29.

Watson, G. "Free Agency." *Journal of Philosophy* 72 (1975): 205–20.

Wegner, D. *The Illusion of Conscious Will.* Cambridge, MA: MIT Press, 2002.

White, J. *Contemporary Moral Problems*, 10th ed. Belmont, CA: Wadsworth, 2012.

Widerker, D. "Libertarianism and Frankfurt's Attack on the Principle of Alternative Possibilities." *Philosophical Review* 104 (1995): 247–61.

Widerker, D., and McKenna, M., eds. *Moral Responsibility and Alternative Possibilities.* London: Ashgate, 2003.

Wolf, S. "Sanity and the Metaphysics of Responsibility." In *Responsibility, Character, and Emotions*, ed. F. Schoeman, 45–64. Cambridge, UK: Cambridge University Press, 1987.

———. *Freedom within Reason.* Oxford: Oxford University Press, 1990.

Wyma, K. "Moral Responsibility and the Leeway for Action." *American Philosophical Quarterly* 34 (1997): 57–70.

Zagzebski, L. *The Dilemma of Freedom and Foreknowledge.* New York: Oxford University Press, 1991.

———. (2004). "Foreknowledge and Free Will." *Stanford Encyclopedia of Philosophy*, rev. 2011, http://plato.stanford.edu/entries/free-will-foreknowledge/.

Index

agent-causal libertarianism, 46–50; criticisms of, 48–50; defenders of, 50; definition of, 46; and dualism, 47; and problem of luck, 47

Aquinas, Thomas, 89

Augustine, St., x, 88

Balaguer, Mark, 59, 72, 74

Berkeley, George, x, 50

Boethius, 89

Brembs, Bjorn, 77–78

Cashmore, Anthony, 77–78

chaos theory, 55–56, 71

Chisholm, Roderick, 50

Clarke, Randolph, 50

compatibilism, 21–36, 45; classical compatibilism, 22, 33; and conditional analysis of "could have done otherwise," 25–26; definition of, 21; and Frankfurt examples, 29–32

consequence argument, 24, 33, 36, 59; and conditional analysis of "could have done otherwise," 25–27; and Frankfurt examples, 29–32; replies to, 25–33

death penalty, 5–6, 13; and deterrence theory, 13; and retributivism, 5–6

Dennett, Daniel, 28, 29, 36

determinism, 8, 45, 65–70; and compatibilism, 21–36; and consequence argument, 24–25; definition of, 8; hard determinism, 8; macro-level determinism, 66–69; and neuroscience, 69–70; and quantum physics, 9, 66

deterrence theory of punishment, 12–13; critique of, 13–14; and death penalty, 12–13

dilemma of determinism, 9–10, 44, 45

divine foreknowledge, problem of, 87–91; Augustinian response to, 88; Boethius' and Aquinas' response to, 88–89; open theist response to, 89–91

dualism, 47

Ekstrom, Laura, 59

evil, problem of, 84–86; free will solution to, 84–86

Festinger, Leon, 75

Flanagan, Owen, 36

forgiveness and excuse, 91

Frankfurt, Harry, 29, 33–36; and analysis of free action, 34–36; and Frankfurt examples, 29–32

Frankfurt examples, 29–32; indeterministic world objection to, 32

Ginet, Carl, 51

God, 84–91

Goetz, Stuart, 51